Goose River Anthology, 2022

Edited by

Deborah J. Benner

Goose River Press
Waldoboro, Maine

Library of Congress Card Number: 2022945793

ISBN: 978-1-59713-248-0 paperback
ISBN: 978-1-59713-249-7 hard cover

First Printing, 2022

Cover photo by Kasey Dow.

Published by
Goose River Press
3400 Friendship Road
Waldoboro, ME 04572
email: gooseriverpress@gmail.com
www.gooseriverpress.com

Authors Included

Ackermann, Helen: Pages 85–86
Babb, Julie: Pages 47 & 126
Barsalou, E. M.: Pages 66 & 196
Belenardo, Sally: Pages 28, 30, 124, 139, 165
Bennett, Thomas Peter: Pages 31 & 97
Bedwell, Mary Ann: Pages 75 & 163
Biegun, Jean: Pages 48, 90, 153
Bishop, Jeffery M.: Page 51
Blackwell, Susan: Pages 95–97
Boey, Brandon Ying Kit: Pages 63 & 194
Bolster, Lou: Pages 83 & 113
Branch, Kristina: Pages 111–112
Braun, Judith L.: Page 125
Brooks, Rebecca: Pages 46–47, 136, 195
Bruney, Sandra: Pages 1–5
Carignan, Georgette: Pages 32 & 142
Carty, Scott: Pages 53–61
Comeau, Philancy: Pages 17–22
Conlon, Sandra: Pages 82–83
Crawford, Mikal: Pages 91–93
D'Alessandro, Adele & Anthony: Pages 203–206
Davis, the late Corinne Eastman: Page 100
de Araujo, Alvaro: Pages 101–107
Decker, Jayne: Pages 88–90
Di Gesu, Gerry: Pages 29–30
Dorman, Janet: Pages 65, 140–141
Edmunds, Mimi: Pages 24–27
Fallon, Thomas: Pages 70, 186–187
Gillespie, John: Page 99
Grey, Judith: Pages 64–65
Hagan, John T: Page 98
Harrington, Ilga Winicov: Pages 143–151

Authors Included

Hart, Olivia C.: Pages 71–73
Hartford, Kitty: Page 84
Hasselman, San D.: Page 94
Herring, Bill: Pages 87, 125, 162
Hill, Andrea: Pages 13 & 161
Hodum, Robert: Pages 33–36
Hubbard, Graydon Dee: Pages 173–182
Julian, Jeanne: Page 38
Kaska, Charles: Page 127
Kearns, Kate: Page 110
Keoughan, Katharina: Pages 115–116
Lafond, Deborah Loomis: Page 108
L'Heureux, Juliana: Pages 119–124
Lid, the late Frank J.: Page 74
Little-Sweat, Sylvia: Pages 31, 66, 112, 130, 163, 166, 169, 196
Lombardo, Elizabeth: Pages 67–68
Lopresto, Rosalie Ann: Pages 137–138
Lord, R. Craig: Pages 49-50
Loughlin, Deborah: Page 37
Manichello, Richard: Pages 197–202
Mathias, Cordula: Pages 7, 117, 164, 187
McClure, Mary: Pages 131–134
Moorehead, P. C.: Pages 22, 135, 171, 183
Moreland, Robert B.: Pages 12, 114, 141, 183
O'Dell, Judy: Pages 189–193
Partington, Cynthia: Pages 14–16
Radoff, Phillip L.: Pages 39–45
Randolph, Patrick T.: Page 206
Ratliff, Kaye Nelson: Pages 155–160
Richards, Bunny L.: Pages 23, 81, 172
Roncone, Margaret: Page 76

Authors Included

Santillo, Stacie: Pages 50 & 152
Sheridan, Grace B.: Pages 61 & 109
Sedgwick, Rosemary: Pages 9–12
Seguin, Marilyn Weymouth: Page 69
Smith, Brenda: Pages 77–81
Staberg, Abby: Pages 8, 99, 184–185
Stewart, Roselyn: Pages 52, 93, 188
Trojan, Peggy: Pages 6, 51, 73, 165
Troyanovich, Steve: Pages 27, 84, 100, 108, 154, 193, 202
Villano, David: Pages 16, 128–129
Wagner, Karen E.: Pages 62–63, 170–171
Wells, Allison Childs: Pages 7, 116, 118
Winchenbaugh, Judy Driscoll: Pages 167–169

Dedicated to
those who came before us.

Special thanks to Sue Campagna for her wonderful help in proofing the book.

Goose River Anthology, 2022

Sandra Bruney
Wadesboro, NC

The Bracelet

She stepped back from the counter just as the clerk turned, a professional smile on her lips.

"Sorry about the phone. Have you decided yet?"

"I'll have to think about it," she said. "It's beautiful, but..."

The clerk's eyes hardened, but her smile never slipped. "Come back any time," she said, her voice cool, already dismissive.

"I will." She had almost reached the door when Mr. Talbot, the young manager of Friedmann's Jewelers, touched her elbow.

"I need you to step into the office," he said. The touch turned into a grip, and she was forced to follow him. "Have a seat," he said, shutting the door behind them.

"I need to get home. My husband—"

"This won't take long. Just return the bracelet and you're free to go, no questions asked."

He wasn't smiling now that there were no customers to observe them. "We'll forget about it. We don't want a disturbance, do we?"

"What are you talking about? I didn't buy the bracelet. It was too expensive." Her voice was high, breathy. *I sound like Jackie Kennedy*, she thought. The manager was so young, though, he probably didn't even know who Jackie was, much less remember her voice.

"I know how much it cost," he said. He might have said more, but the door opened and the clerk came inside, a policeman behind her.

"I didn't tell you to call the police," Mr. Talbot said to clerk.

"Rubies and diamonds set in platinum?" she said, raising one perfect eyebrow. "Of course, I called the police."

Sandra Bruney
Wadesboro, NC

"You're positive you saw her take it?"

"Not exactly. She was looking at the tray when I was called to the telephone. When I came back, she said she'd changed her mind and I put the tray back in the case. It was then I saw the empty space and buzzed your office."

The officer spoke for the first time. "I need you to empty your purse, ma'am."

Shaking, she turned her purse upside down over the desk and shook it. Keys, wallet, checkbook, a small wad of tissue, a lipstick, and a pack of breath mints scattered over the polished oak. The officer checked each item, opening the wallet, sliding back the tin lid of the box and running a finger through the tiny white mints, uncapping the lipstick.

"Surely you don't think I managed to hide a bracelet in a tube of lipstick," she said, her tone more amazed than shocked.

"You'd be surprised," he answered. "May I see your coat?"

She slipped it off and watched in helpless anger as he thrust his hand into each pocket, pulling out her gloves and feeling each finger in turn.

"That's enough." She could feel the heat in her cheeks, although her body felt icy cold. Looking straight at Mr. Talbot, she said, "If you insist on continuing this charade, then I insist on this officer taking me downtown and having a female deputy do a strip search, or whatever you call it. Then, when she's through, I intend to go directly across the street to my attorney's office and have him sue this store for harassment and whatever else he can think of." She turned to the officer. "And then, I'll have him sue the town for false arrest."

"All right, there's no need to be upset, Mrs. ...?" the officer said in a soothing tone, as if talking to a child.

"Mrs. Carmody. Mrs. William J. Carmody."

The words echoed in the sudden silence. She could see Mr. Talbot's eyes widen, the clerk's smile freeze, a dark red line in a suddenly ashen face. She didn't need to add Bill

Sandra Bruney
Wadesboro, NC

Carmody of Carmody Manufacturing, the town's biggest and only major employer. They knew that, just as she knew Bill Dean was a night-shift foreman and Jean Talbot was head of purchasing. Chances were good that the policeman had relatives working at Carmody, also.

Mr. Talbot found his voice first. "I'm very sorry. Apparently, Mrs. Dean has made an error."

The clerk's mouth worked, but she said nothing. She looked away, her shoulders sagging in defeat.

The officer cleared his throat. "No charges, then?"

He received an "are you kidding" glare for his stupidity.

"Guess you're free to go," the officer said. He touched his cap in salute. "Sorry for the trouble, ma'am."

Mr. Talbot silently held the door open and she sailed through, her head high, her coat draped over her arm in spite of the cold air that met her when she exited the shop. Only when she reached her black Lexus did she begin to shake. The tremors started deep inside and made their way to the muscles in her arms and legs. Tears welled in her eyes and she felt bile rise in her throat. She willed the nausea away. No one would see her break down, especially that arrogant clerk. She had never been so embarrassed in her life. Thank God none of her friends had been there. She couldn't have borne that.

She'd tell Bill, and he would soothe and pet her until the horrid incident began to fade away. She'd let those awful people think he would repay them for her humiliation by hurting their families, but they didn't know Bill. He'd never do anything like that. He was a kind man, so kind...

On second thought, she wouldn't tell him at all. She'd caused him so much grief these past months. She could spare him this—this *fiasco*, for that was what it was. She looked up to see the policeman staring at her car. He started toward her and she quickly put the Lexus in gear and pulled out of the parking space.

One thing was certain, she would never shop there again.

Sandra Bruney
Wadesboro, NC

If that clerk hadn't ignored her to chat on the telephone to her friend, she might have even bought that stupid bracelet. Too bad—their loss.

She felt her self-confidence return and the trembling stopped. She must not let this one incident ruin her day. Shopping had always cheered her up before and she tried to regain her earlier lightheartedness by deliberately putting the memory of the past fifteen minutes behind her, where it belonged. By the time she got home, she felt quite happy again.

Once inside, she went to her bedroom and threw her purse on the bed. The coat followed and spilled over the coverlet, the dark brown lining shining like melted chocolate in the afternoon sunlight. There was a tiny tear in the seam of the right-hand pocket. It was a wonder the policeman's blunt, sausage-like fingers hadn't widened it further. She ran her hand over the smooth silk along the hem.

She looked up when she heard the door slam and Bill's footsteps on the parquet floor.

Smiling in anticipation, she walked with quick strides to the living room.

He turned around when he heard her and she could have laughed at the look of surprise on his face—a look that turned to joy.

"You're dressed!" he said.

"I could hardly go to the beauty shop in my bathrobe, could I?" She patted her hair with a little pout. "Or didn't you notice?"

"I noticed." His voice was hoarse. "It looks real nice, honey."

"Thanks." She shrugged. "I was getting tired of it getting into my eyes, and then I noticed how gray it was getting. Cecille did a nice job, don't you think? I'm lucky she could work me in. A good color job takes a lot of time."

"I hope you burned the bathrobe."

She smiled. "No, but I put it in the trash."

Sandra Bruney
Wadesboro, NC

His eyes told her what he was thinking: six long months of seeing her in nothing but that faded blue robe, her hair carelessly tied back, her eyes vacant.

"It's gone," she said, and she didn't mean the robe.

"I guess that new prescription finally did the trick."

She smiled back. She hadn't taken it. It had been the look in Bill's eyes that morning, the slow defeated way he walked to the door, that had forced her to pick up the phone and call Cecille.

"Maybe," she said.

"Something cheered you up, anyway. This calls for a celebration. What say we go out for dinner? I'll make a reservation at Santini's. That okay?"

"Fine."

He took out his iPhone and began running his finger over the screen, turning his back on the glare from the window.

She crossed the room to draw the drapes against the evening sun. Before she did, she held her arm up to the light pouring through the window, admiring the glittering rainbow that encircled her wrist and cast a prism of dancing red and white reflections on the opposite wall.

Peggy Trojan
Brule, WI

The Trestle

When I was nine
the world was at war.
I had nightmares
about that at times
but the scariest act
I could think of
was venturing onto
the railroad trestle
high over the river,
no railings.
The boys dared us
to walk across.
In the middle you could see
the rushing water
through the ties.
It made you dizzy.
If a locomotive had
come shooting from town
we would have had to lie down
between the rails
and let the whole train run
over the top of us,
like in the movies.

Cordula Mathias
Trevett, ME

Winter Olympics 2014

Broken temperature records.
Pipes laid and broken.
Roads and venues built
In record time.
Bones cracked or fractured,
Doping rules broken.
New records set.
Broken promises.
The treaty broken:
Tanks breaching the border.
War has broken out.
A country is broken up
Tomorrow.
Although,
We don't know that yet.

***

Allison Childs Wells
Gardiner, ME

May

Apple trees point
pink white. Yellow faces
of daffodils, cardinals
in full red song.

I wake, your arms around me.

Sweet green returning
to the fallow field.

Abby Staberg
Brunswick, ME

How It Ends

We awaken to a shimmering sun
struck by the stillness in the air.

We listen for the murmur of the desert
but hear nothing.

Sagebrush scoots across the sand
without a *whoosh.*

We want the wind to whistle
but it won't.

Birds fly here and there.
They are hushed silhouettes with no purpose.

A snake slides under a dusty rock.
There is no hiss.

Afternoon falters and falls to its knees
in silence.

The horizon swallows the sun.
Millions of stars seek the darkening void.

A hopeful moon arises
to no welcoming howls.

I stifle an anguished mournful cry.
It echoes in your eyes.

Rosemary Sedgwick
Boxborough, MA

First Trip to Winter Harbor

It was 1955. My father had returned from the Pacific ten years before, when I was just a "tidbit" in my mother's womb. There were now four children. I was the oldest at nine, my youngest sister was a baby. We lived on top of each other in a small house in Durham, North Carolina, where my father was the minister of an Episcopal church. Summers were sweltering and long.

One day that spring we had unfamiliar company crowded around our kitchen table. They had come down from the north to interview my father for the job of summer pastor at a chapel in Maine. At the time, I thought my three-year-old brother ruined the interview by spilling a full glass of milk across the table. However, my parents mopped it up in a heartbeat, cheerfully resuming the conversation as if nothing untoward had happened. My father was hired soon after.

Maine was a very long way away and a very big land mass on the map. My mother identified Winter Harbor as a dot on the Down East coastline. "It would take us two nights and days to get there," she explained.

That first summer, we traveled the fifteen hundred miles in our old black Ford sedan. When I think of my parents setting off with the four of us in that car, I have to say, they were of a doughty generation. I was bedded down on the back seat. My father had built a wooden platform spanning the car floor below me; my next youngest sister slept there. My brother hung in a canvas rack above her, and the baby traveled in a lap up front. Our luggage was piled in a heap on the roof, and covered—in a last-minute flash of inspiration—with the shower curtain from the bathroom. It flapped all the way to Winter Harbor.

We left at dusk and drove through the night. At odd hours in the darkness, I was aware of the car pulling over for

Rosemary Sedgwick
Boxborough, MA

gas, for a change of drivers, for whispered, urgent, infuriated consultations over the map. Had they missed the Tappan Zee? It took me years to realize that the Tappan Zee is a bridge near New York City. In my dreamy state I imagined us looking for a landmark, maybe a windmill, in some sort of Dutchlike countryside with tulips and cows.

When we woke in the morning, my mother had a surprise for us, henceforth to be known on our Maine journeys as "Mother's Bag of Tricks." The bags for me and my six year old sister contained crayons and coloring books, cards, travel games, chewing gum. We were astounded. It was like Christmas. My parents were in wonderful moods, singing rounds of "White Coral Bells," and "Down Yonder in the Green Grove." It got even better when we stopped in Poughkeepsie and had our first meal in a restaurant. Mother knew the place from her days at Vassar, and had promised us each a Vassar Devil dessert. It proved worthy of its name. I could hardly believe the tantalizing heap of devil's food cake, vanilla ice cream, hot fudge and marshmallow sauce delivered to me on a dessert plate.

We stayed the night—six in a motor lodge room—visited with an old friend of my mother's the next day, then took to the road as the sun set. A gray dawn roused me. My parents were silent up front, and my siblings were still asleep. I looked out the car window at a grim landscape. For miles, there was nothing but somber evergreen forest and slabs of rock where the road had been blasted through. Occasionally, we would pass a burnt-out clearing, with wasted black trunks of trees sticking up from the charred ground. For miles, we drove alone through this vast land, the only car on the two-lane highway, the only moving thing.

The turnoff down route 186, which would lead us to the coast, was unpromising, more of the same. Somewhere along the road, though, the sun came up and sent warm, hopeful rays into our car. When we rolled down our windows, the Maine air astonished us. In the thick heat of southern summers, we could barely breathe at all. Now our lungs filled with the crisp cool breath of a million acres of Maine pine and sea.

The sea breeze got stronger and stronger, and then suddenly the road came to an end at a T intersection. Before us was a picture-postcard Maine harbor, glinting in the early sun. On our left, the road led by a bunch of small, trim buildings to a pier, where lobster boats idled in the tide. We followed the road on our right, past the post office and supermarket, through the village and around to the chapel of St. Christopher by the Sea.

We couldn't believe our luck. Though modest compared to the mansions (called "cottages") of the regular summer people, the chapel rectory was luxurious compared to our house in Durham. There was a separate bedroom for each child, and a wide front porch which served as an outdoor anteroom for all our comings and goings.

In those days, children too old for babysitting were free to roam. The only formally scheduled activities were sailboat races. (My family didn't own a boat, but we were invited to crew.) I remember walking to the village for penny candy and hiding it from my parents and siblings. I remember fishing for pollock off the dock, and then (stupidly and cruelly) fishing for sea gulls with chunks of pollock. I remember setting myself the challenge of making my way alone, at age eleven, around the rocky point of the Winter Harbor peninsula. It was dangerous; I clambered over rocks slippery with seaweed and clutched at crevices in steep cliffs, waves crashing below me. About halfway around, I lost my nerve but by then it would have been harder to retrace my steps than continue forward. I didn't tell my parents about that outing either.

They had their own fun and freedoms. A charming couple, my parents were included in all the adult activities (except golf, but they weren't golfers anyway), and they made good friends among the second and third generation summer people who were generally less wealthy than their forebears

Rosemary Sedgwick
Boxborough, MA

and more clever. Two of these composed a verse of the Yacht Club song in honor of my parents:

Our rockbound coast received a burst of southern charm
When Tom and Romey arrived with a child in every arm,
And if Romey keeps coming up with bundles of good news,
Then we think that Tom will yet succeed in filling up the pews.

It was a small chapel. My father had no trouble filling it without adding another sleeping berth to the old Ford sedan.

***

Robert B. Moreland
Pleasant Prairie, WI

Called Away

No, I do not ask you why
when I see you slipping away
quietly to that place you go;
far from the busy world to your space.

How hard being one yet still two,
individual souls entwined.
Love that binds but that still trusts,
unique hearts flourishing alone.

Please don't doubt my love for you,
even though I seem so distant—
working through the trials of my soul;
renewed to hold you again.

Moreland, R.B. (2022) "Called Away" *Poetry Quarterly* Fall 2021 in press.

Andrea Hill
Jonesboro, ME

Game On

November leaves spin,
lost in dervish dance,
deciduous planets swirl
with north wind updrafts,
sprinkle as stars
over backyard galaxies
before December's eye teeth
tear open winter and
the whole cosmos
eyes the solstice...

Ice pellets forged in
Ullr's arctic cauldron
pierce weathered cheeks and
ungloved calloused hands like
arrows from his quiver.
A pagan Norse god, he struts his stuff.
Glazed trees pop in his dark grasp.
Thoughts spark as swords,
rivals in a clash of wills,
hope as hollow as fear,
despair's furnace.

Cindy Partington
Dallas Center, IA

At Your Fingertips

having started the sofa and your hand on fire
with your cigarette
without noticing
having fallen backwards down the basement steps
as well as off the front porch
your reality shifted
your new home—a former stately mansion
with its repurposed rooms
each a refuge of adjustable hospital beds
and treasured momentos of previous existences
happier and stronger times
I marveled the photo you chose
standing by your new curly-haired blond bride
ready to take on all things
the tall thin bespeckled and very handsome you

finding purpose
you shuffled on your iffy Parkinson's legs
going bed to bed by appointment
to read aloud classics, Westerns, poetry or
sappy romance novels
chosen by your bedridden comrades
filling their emptiness and isolation
filling also your need
to feel useful
to feel worthwhile
you helped muffle the harsh realities
of God's waiting room

when blurry shadows
increasingly masked your eyes and world

(con't.)

Cindy Partington
Dallas Center, IA

taking away your daily rounds of reading aloud
you tried still to make your way
stumbling through the halls
and friendly caretakers curbed your wanderings

your decision made
at first no one noticed you'd quit eating
you threw your false teeth into wastebaskets
again and again
until weakness triumphed
and family was called

I went with your son, my father
but was told you didn't want me coming in to see you
I waited while Dad sat with you

and when you'd taken your leave
Dad told me of your well-worn small suitcase
propped open on a chair in the corner
with postcards I'd sent you
pinned to its lining
and related
how you'd struggled to voice some message
tears in your eyes
valuable beyond measure
because you wanted to say it
your mouth no longer responded to your thoughts
the alphabet board was lifted
from its place
you took a moment
unable to condense your heart's message
into a soundless string of letters
your fingertips lifted slightly from the bed
and were met by your son's
clearly conveying your message

Cindy Partington
Dallas Center, IA

I think of you often Pop
I think of you often Dad

***

David Villano
Jefferson, ME

Greeting a Tree When I Am Old

I'm sorry...
I cannot recall your name.
(Or mine. I think.)
But we've met before.

I don't recall the color of your leaves in autumn
or the shape of the nuts you bear
or from which crook
in your trunk
(wait...is it that one?)
many years ago
a young boy of maybe ten
(Did I know him?)
once stood and crouched
and dared to jump—
and then...*off he went!*—
tumbling to the ground,
laughing, as I did.

Yes...I'm certain now.
We've met before.

Philancy Comeau
Rockland, ME

Passion on the Colorado Plains

Alone in her cabin, Ellen Holloway rises with the sun. Her heart races with anticipation because today, she will learn her fate. She flips back her handmade quilt and steps over to the bedroom window.

Her parents harnessed their gelding and left for Fort Morgan yesterday on their annual spring trip for farm supplies. A broad smile brightens her beige complexion as she steps lightly onto the front porch. She tightly wraps her nightgown around her chilled body and takes in the vast honey-toned prairie and a herd of antelope grazing on a corner of their homestead. Over the rise to the west is the dark silhouette of jagged peaks poking into the cobalt sky. Her suitor, Tall Timber, calls them the Mountains of Stone. Her people call them the Rocky Mountains.

Ellen changes into her work clothes, a now ratty dress her mother used to wear to church, and takes two wooden buckets from under the porch walking the few yards to the North Platte River, which meanders through their homestead. The spring runoff fills the river basin with rushing water, and by summer's end, the river will be nothing more than a trickle.

She approaches the tumbling water cautiously, fearful of falling in and nearly drowning as she did years ago. The thin fabric of her dress does not protect her knees from the sharp pebbles while crawling over to the riverbank to fill the buckets. Lying on her belly, she reaches through the tall grasses to scoop water.

After backing away from the riverbank on her hands and knees, she stands, brushes off her dress, and runs her hands over her burning knees. When she picks up the buckets, the wire handles dig into her palms. She walks slow and steady up the well-worn path as it snakes its way up to the

Philancy Comeau
Rockland, ME

barn that sits on a knoll over the river. Her shoulders strain under the extra weight, and her calves burn as she climbs. She enters the barn to water and feed the workhorses, cows, and chickens as she does every morning.

Ellen's youthful giddiness and excitement for the day ahead turn into anxiety because she knows her greatest desire will anger and disgust her parents. She has kept her passion for Tall Timber a secret to allow their love to bud without prejudice. Last week, he professed his desire for marriage but insisted he must ask the chief for permission because that is their way. She never thought to ask why.

Her hand covers her sour stomach as bile threatens to rise into her mouth. She leaves the animals, crosses the wild grasses growing between the barn and the cabin, and enters the kitchen. She eats the heel of a loaf of bread, her mother's recommended cure for indigestion.

Ellen puts her nervous energy to work, giving the cabin a thorough cleaning by sweeping, making her bed, and emptying the ashes from the fireplace. She stands with one hand on her hip and the other holding a broom, smiling broadly, hoping that her efforts will put her mother in a good mood when she arrives home the next day.

After washing her face and brushing her long, golden locks, she puts on her favorite frock with the pansy print and matching bonnet, gifts from her parents for her sixteenth birthday last summer.

When Ellen leaves the cabin, she takes her water flask from the peg next to the door but forgets to grab her rifle in her haste. She carefully steps through the swaying grasses accompanied by a light breeze and cawing crows circling overhead. Out of sight of her homestead, she climbs a short, steep hill digging the toes of her boots into the soft dirt. Sharp blades of grass threaten to cut her palms as she pulls herself up onto the plateau. At the top, she stops to catch her breath and scan the expansive land owned by the Arapaho Nation, where one blustery autumn day, she met

Philancy Comeau
Rockland, ME

the love of her life, Tall Timber.

The plateau is flat as a griddle dotted with sage, scrub brush, and rattlesnakes, some ten feet long. If bitten by a rattler, she will suffer a horrible death, and her body will be torn to pieces by scavengers. Not a pretty picture. In tune with her surroundings, she walks with purpose, her arms swinging at her side. Under her bonnet, she cannot help but smile in anticipation that her greatest desire will come true today, that the chief will allow them to marry.

In the distance is a giant boulder the Arapahos call "Fallen Rock" because it looks like it fell from the sky. It's a large red, angular bump on otherwise flat land. Walking along, a rattling sound buzzes in her ears. She stops mid-step, foot dangling in the air. Her heart bangs in her chest. To her right, the grass sways in the still air. A rattler's head rises above the prairie, tongue flicking. Moments later, it slithers away in the opposite direction. She studies every tuft of grass and debris surrounding her to ensure she has not accidentally stepped into a nest.

Ellen searches the horizon for any distant movement and sees what appears to be a moving wall but is a large herd of buffalo roaming the range. Disappointed, she plops down on the large straw mat woven by Tall Timber that he had pinned to the ground like a teepee. They made this little patch of prairie their special meeting place to share their love and huddle against the bigotry of their peoples. Today, he won't be coming alone. He will be with Chief Red Cloud and other men within his tribe.

Cool water from her flask coats her mouth and stomach. Her skin prickles in the intense dry heat. Peeking out from under her bonnet at the faraway horizon, Ellen spots tribe members coming her way. At this distance, she can't tell what tribe they belong to. Fear of Pawnee warriors that travel through the plains looking for humans to sacrifice puts her on alert. Ellen looks behind her, where she usually leans her shotgun against the rock, and it's not there. Beads of sweat cool her forehead. Jumping to her feet, she runs to the other side of the boulder out of view. Peeking around the side, they are galloping towards her, getting closer. Their solid and large bodies riding high on their horses tell her that they are Arapaho and not the Pawnee, who are small in stature and live nearly naked. Exhaling loudly, her muscles slacken with relief, and then she steps out from behind the rock.

They are getting close enough to make out Chief Red Cloud's large feather headdress and spear that he carries in his left hand. He is accompanied by six men in a "V" formation. Passion burns within her at the sight of Tall Timber to the chief's right.

Dust rises from under the horses' hooves dirtying the cloudless sky. As they near, the thunderous noise of the galloping horses pounds in her ears. The chief, riding point, raises his spear far over his head and stops just a few yards away. His horse rears up in a show of strength. The others stop slightly behind and to the side of the chief.

Ellen steps away from the boulder with her hands clasped at her waist. She looks out from under her bonnet, nods at the chief as is custom, and smiles shyly at her lover.

A pained smile rises on Tall Timber's bronze face making his teeth and eyes stand out. He wears only a loincloth and chaps over a sculpted body capable of meeting any task. Hairless, except for the black braids reaching to his shoulders, his skin is irresistibly smooth. Ellen stifles a nervous giggle.

Tall Timber dismounts and stands barefoot within inches of her, gently holding her hands in his. His callouses are rough against her tender skin. They look into each other's eyes. Her pounding heart aches when she recognizes sorrow and resignation in his chiseled features.

"This is way it must be," he whispers tearfully. "Cannot be another way, but my heart be with you." He turns and walks away with his tomahawk banging against his chaps.

Pain radiates from her heart throughout her young body.

Philancy Comeau
Rockland, ME

Blood rushes to her head, making her dizzy. Her shaking knees can no longer support her, so she falls onto them, sobbing into her hands and crying out, “No! Please God, no!” Her pained voice echoes in her ears. She falls forward, her fingers grasping the hard dirt. “No. Please. I must be with my love.”

Chief Red Cloud dismounts, holding his spear. His bison-hide fringed chaps and wrap-around shirt are decorated with animal bones and polished beads. He approaches her, standing with the toes of his moccasins beneath her hanging head. “Do not allow ache in heart. It destroy you.”

She gazes at him, sitting back on her heels, squinting from the sun’s glare. “Please, we love each other so. I don’t want to live without him.”

“Stand. I may speak,” the chief commands.

Her body shakes with despair, her mouth twitching as she rises to her feet.

“Tall Timber speaks of love for you. He sincere.”

Her head hangs, tears drop from her pale blue eyes onto the parched soil.

The chief continues, “Tradition requires I seek Great Spirit, our Creator. In sweat lodge, I receive answer. A vision. Tall Timber, strong warrior, and future chief. No marry white woman. Squaw.”

Looking into the chief’s eyes, she wipes tears from her face and screeches, “I’ll kill myself. I will!”

“You young,” he states in a flat tone.

She grabs the chief’s arm, and he gently removes her hand. “Please. We love each other. You can’t do this.”

“Creator’s decision. He make, not me. Tall Timber find happiness with Arapaho squaw.”

“Ask again. Won’t you ask again? Maybe the Creator doesn’t know we’re in love.”

“Creator knows best,” he says, turning toward his men. “Must go.”

Ellen runs to Tall Timber, stands next to his horse, and

Philancy Comeau
Rockland, ME

hugs his chapped leg smelling leather and sweat. She looks up at her beloved with tear-filled eyes.

"This is way it must be," he says, stony-faced, but his watery eyes and tender voice reveal his true feelings. He frees his leg from her grasp, pulls on his reins, and turns away.

Her hands cover her wet face, and her breaths are shallow and fast. "No. No. Come back. No." She collapses to the ground at the departing sound of horse hooves and the nearby rattling of a snake's tail.

***

P. C. Moorehead
North Lake, WI

The Drama of Life

My life is a mystery, and you, friends,
you are the theater, you are the audience.

Played out before you are all the acts:
the good, the bad, the left out.

My mystery is now nearing its end.
There are some acts left.

What will they be?
Good, bad, left out.

I do not know the solution to my mystery.
You know the solution.

You are the theater, the audience.
You are the drama of my life.

Bunny L. Richards
Trescott Twp., ME

Descending into Darkness

Mary says "You know how it is,
some days are good, others
not so much."

Beth won't talk to her,
blames it all on Mary.
(Home on the lake empty.)

Pat has his own problems,
uncle missing, bio Dad disowned.
First to see Ken,
what was left, that is.

(Took the kids fishing there.)

Now, leaves and apples fallen,
swing set lists to one side.
Someone put a bullet in the kayak

Can't remember when.

Mimi Edmunds
Rockport, ME

Water and Complexity: An Album

Photograph: Free—at 13
At Rocky Point the sun slips down behind the sea.
I photograph Eliza backlit in silhouette,
Arms in the air, skinny legs planted firmly
In the sand. I feel the joy I cannot see on her face,
An aura framed by the sun at her back.
I see the freedom only a 13-year-old body can express—
Tripping along the edge of the sea.
I was letting her go—
And she was letting go,
Flirting with the rippling surf between her toes
On the Baja at Rocky Point.

Photograph: Foam and Seaweed—at 2
She sits square in a pool of seaweed and foam
Lathering her silky skin in the sun
While floating lily pads frame and tickle her little body.
Between the edge of the surf and the dunes
A Buddha baby, she sits in a luscious bath of vanilla surf,
Her tiny hands banging puddles like cymbals.

At night when she would cry,
The sound of running water soothed.
Bathing in the bathroom sink she
Paints her likeness on steamy mirrors.
Warm water working its magic
To calm and delight,
To fascinate and explore.

Mimi Edmunds
Rockport, ME

Photograph: Diving—at 10

Leaping high into the air
Curling her body into a ball she dives into the pool,
Slapping the water with a mushroom splash,
It is her tenth birthday—
She goes under, then up and bursting out—
Only to do it again—and again.

Photograph: With starfish and Big Page—at 11

Summer at the eastern tip of Canada—
She plucks starfish off the rocks
When the tide flows out too fast,
Walking gingerly on slippery rocks
With grandfather Big Page, just the two of them.
Engrossed in this marine wonderland ~
A confluence of four bodies of water,
The St Croix, two bays, and the sea.
They bend over to reach down
And muck and muse with the verdant life
That lives between the rocks and weeds ~
At the edge of the Passamaquoddy Bay ~
That feeds into the Bay of Fundy ~
Where whales play.

She collects a bucket of clamshells,
muscles, and one prize starfish.
Showing off her captives in her hands,
she stands ankle deep in the tidal shore
in red boots, cut-off jean shorts,
and a tank top—hinting at little breast buds.
"Time for a training bra, Mom!" She laughs at herself,
"The boys call me a joke—they say I'm an
'obstacle illusion,' "
And laughs again.

Mimi Edmunds
Rockport, ME

Photograph: Fishing in the "Lollipop"—at 12
They head out in the dingy to a red and white lobster pot
Called "Lollipop" ~ to fish for hours,
catching nothing. The grandfather never good with children
Befriends his last grandchild with brown skin.

Photograph: Maryland by the Bay—at 14
Today Eliza is blind. She goes swimming
in the warm Chesapeake Bay
for the first time since a virus attacked her brain
in September, a year ago, taking her sight and memory.
Unabashed, she leaps off the dock
like she did at ten.
Smiling for the photographer, she looks sideways—
not knowing where the beach is.

Sitting in shallow water just like at two—
"Come on in, Mom," wanting to splash me like before.
She is at home in the water again ~ it soothing
caressing ~ sliding over her body ~
Her face seems to light up with a memory,
Of surf, rocks, and starfish with Big Page.
But she never wants to go under again.

Painting: "Sun, wind, and the sea"
Today water is complicated, carrying
Fear—
Of the unknown,
Of letting go of what she can no longer see.
Instead of steamy mirrors to draw on,
She runs a brush over a canvas
Splashing large strokes with fairylike flicks of her wrist
painting sensations, memories
In *Seascape. Sun, Water, and Sea.*
A self-portrait.
Or is it just complex?

Steve Troyanovich
Florence, NJ

...and the leaves sing into the wind

for Rodolfo Alonso

i feel your absence
beyond the stolen moments
of muted words...your incandescent voice
embraces through the silence
of your hands

the earth still sings
dancing around delirious stars
and suspended rhythms...their cadence
holding that impenetrable alphabet
of lost tomorrows keeping oblivion warm

time dreams...your mouth closes
its eyes...memory falls into a canto
of loneliness drifting through the soft petals
of crabapple snow

Sally Belenardo
Branford, CT

Lucky Finds

Three shallow bowls on a table
in a second-hand shop—

milk white, with a thin, French blue line
around the scalloped rims—

useful underneath potted plants
on kitchen windowsill.

The herbs outgrew their flowerpots;
the bowls were stored away

until a little French poodle,
malnourished and abused,

came to stay. Now the bowls serve her
dog food of gourmet kind:

filet mignon, Spring vegetables,
on which she dines. She won't

starve for love anymore, and she
eats from dinnerware fine.

Gerry Di Gesu
Chatham, MA

Celebration

I just finished reviewing a collection of wedding photos posted online from my daughter's wedding and I can't stop grinning. There is joy in every picture, on every face. This was not a wedding—this was a celebration of life. A coming together of families and friends, ideas and relationships forged yesterday and fifty years ago, a sharing of life stories. It was an amazing day.

And it happened on April 14, 2007—the one day the sun was shining after more than a week of bleak and chilly weather and the day before a northeaster arrived on Cape Cod and lasted longer than expected. Draw your own conclusions but I know it was God smiling on this special couple who have worked through seven long years to forge a loving relationship that grows stronger daily.

In New Jersey, weddings are often "productions" in which obscene amounts of money are spent, usually to impress others for one day. You would be amazed at the number of parents who have taken home equity loans to pay for their daughters' weddings. They're orchestrated by wedding planners and wedding hosts at the reception which is usually a formal sit-down dinner. The day follows a regimented plan with little spontaneity and joy. Not for Nancy and Matt. They wanted a wedding that was simple and joyful. And it was.

The guests were an eclectic mix of young and old, physicians and attorneys, carpenters and fishermen. We were afraid the more reticent New England friends might be overwhelmed by a large contingent with the reputed New Jersey attitude, but what a wonderful blending it was. Everyone mixed and chatted and laughed together. I saw folks dancing I've never seen dance before. The music never stopped. And Nancy never stopped. Whenever anyone had asked her about her wedding, her answer always was "I want to dance." The

Gerry Di Gesu
Chatham, MA

atmosphere was warm and embracing with clear twinkling lights bordering the room and bright flowers providing pockets of welcome on each table. The bar bill was much less than expected and the owner said he couldn't remember when guests finished almost all the food at the buffet. Success.

I stood looking at the whirling folks on the dance floor, listening to the chatter and laughter around me and was filled with joy beyond belief. And then I looked at my two adopted sons and their sister who was born into our family when they were eight and six years old. They were dancing in a circle, roaring with laughter. I thought—how amazing—that three sets of parents brought these children into the world and here they are—one family sharing great happiness. The thought startled me because I never think of my children in that way and I wondered why I did at that moment. Then I realized that their "blending" was the icing on the cake. The perfect example of everyone who had come together with such joy for this day for a true celebration of life.

***

Sally Belenardo
Branford, CT

Unclean

What is it about
money that makes people dirt
poor and filthy rich?

Thomas Peter Bennett
Silver Spring, MD

Audubon's Florida Dream

John James Audubon dreamed
of exploring Florida after it had been
popularized by William Bartram's TRAVELS,
and natural history discoveries of others.

Audubon was inspired to focus
on paintings and descriptions of
Birds of Florida
for his great work in progress,

Audubon's epiphany culminated in
his exploration of Florida
in Bartram's, and other's
tracks—and further
south to Key West—
        seeking new, unique American birds.

***

Sylvia Little-Sweat
Wingate, NC

Carolina Wren

Tail high in the wind,
The wren brings twigs, moss, and grass—
Lines her nest with new Spring green.

Georgette Carignan
Limerick, ME

The Trees Are Talking Today

It is an old stand of trees.
Trunks have fallen
Into crazy zig zags.
Like airborne
Pick up sticks.
Z's and X's everywhere.

On a windy day
The trees talk to me.
Trunks lean on each other
Like a violin bow.
The sound is loud
I look for wounded geese.

Then I remember
It is the trees.
Barks chafed raw to their tender pulp.
They want to be heard.
They have a voice.
And I listen.

A performance.
Of wind
And wood.
The music is there
For all who are willing
To
Stop.
To
Listen.

Robert Hodum
Sound Beach, NY

The Captain's Vessel

A beacon, malignant, and eternal
Silently stands on Sweet Water Hill,
A fetid asylum, graffitied and dank,
Assiduously biding its time,
With panther-like stealth.

Silhouettes on its clapboard
In the gloaming's failing sun,
Convene each evening,
Somewhere off the Hudson
In the hamlet of Crum Creek Run.

This tombstone of a house,
No impartial observer here,
When its tipping point is reached,
Swallows vagrants, intruders, and the tiniest thrill seekers
From their heads to their feet.

This sentinel's
Stained-wall profiles
Witness the passing of the unwitting, complicit, sighted or
blind,
Those who stumble into its clutches
Leave nothing but their shadowy shapes
And moldering trinkets behind.

Wind's sly hand pulls curtains aside,
A tease to any who foolishly push through this slack-jawed
door,
And roam inside.
Through the cobwebs, rancid air, and centuries of debris,
It's core, so ravenously deranged, longs to be free.

Robert Hodum
Sound Beach, NY

Not a creak or a whimper,
No turns of a rusty hinge,
While a slew of gangling dynamos,
With miniature crane legs
Run wild over the rusting strings of the worm-eaten spinet,
Playing mazurkas, nocturnes, sonatas and fugues.

Huddled tight,
shadow people reprise their sorrowful tales,
While dried leaves like mice fleeing spiked heels
Swoosh down hickory floors worn bare,
And whisk away with their knotty tails
Snippets of fabric and hair,
Remnants of the doomed who vanished here.

In August's squally twilight, they'd disappear.
Unlikely to be found any time soon,
Planted deep under the gardens where belladonna blooms.
The hands of the owner, their fate, secured.
This, her answer to nocturnal voices that since childhood
Only she could hear,
Voices whose existence others derided, yet came to fear.

This scarecrow house
In all its glory,
Sings odes to its guests and their sordid stories,
Long past alive, their essence captured in silhouette,
Over plaster walls, this cyclorama of phantoms extends.
Lost souls all, mourned in the hamlet of Crum Creek Run,
This vessel for evil evermore
Lurks in the shadows on Sweet Water Hill,
Waiting for you to come.

Postscript:

Found in a roll-top desk, this neatly folded leaf of verses,

Robert Hodum
Sound Beach, NY

written by a well-trained hand, represents what is believed to be the last writings of Miss Joan Louise Sanders, eccentric heir to the fortune of Captain James Lionel Sanders. The captain, distinguished veteran of the battle of Honey Hill, South Carolina in 1864, and sole owner and operator of the steamboat *G.A.Custer*, was a lifelong resident of the Hudson Valley.

The *Custer*, with 260 feet on the keel, contained 105 staterooms and ran between Kingston and Albany, servicing the ports and communities along the Hudson River. Captain Sanders and his steamboat enjoyed considerable notoriety, but not without controversy. Several accounts of unsolved disappearances of passengers, and rumors of strange and unnatural goings-on, attributed to the eccentric clientele that associated with the captain, overshadowed his endeavors.

Though the captain invested his time and treasure in his steamboat company, he poured his soul into the family's manor and its maze-like gardens. He and his spouse, Catherine, sponsored evening soirées that culminated in walks through the Sanders' labyrinth. Their out-of-town guests, aided by the light of hundreds of lanterns, proceeded along the intersecting paths and through tree-covered clearings to the cavernous gazebo that the captain's manservant had built. This structure enshrined stone benches and a granite altar under which ran a mountain stream. Beneath its fresh water current, on October nights, the stain of a curved-edged dagger would appear. Rumors of strange rituals fed the locals' appetite for more salacious and questionable activities.

Catherine de Windt Sanders, whose family hailed from Rotterdam, was known to practice New World Dutch folk rituals, and met regularly with locals of similar mind. At the homeowner's request, she'd conceal talismans under floorboards or in walls to ward off *kwade geesten*, evil spirits. Catherine specialized in the preparation of *witch bottles*,

Robert Hodum
Sound Beach, NY

which she filled with human teeth, small metallic implements, desiccated animal paws or tails, and shreds of colorful clothing.

Captain Sanders passed in the winter of 1893, leaving his considerable fortune to Catherine who continued to operate the family business until her demise in 1910. As per her written request, bent pins and nails, locks of children's hair, broken toys, and a pair of worn shoes lined her sarcophagus.

The *Custer,* moored to a dock at Rondout Creek, off the Hudson River, burned to the waterline in 1911.

Their only child, Joan Louise, inhabited the Sanders' mansion for the next fifty-three years. A recluse and millionaire, this accomplished pianist's music could be heard throughout the estate. Locals believed that she had a lifelong association with an older, gentleman gardener who lived on the manor's grounds.

In 1964, a local constable, responding to reports of strange lights and screams, found her in the estate's garden, collapsed near a belladonna bush. The gardener, purple faced, dangled upside down from a shagbark hickory, with a noose cinched around his left ankle, like *The Hanged Man* of the Tarot.

The coroner, cognizant of the toxicology of her poisoning, signed the official death certificate that stated, *Death due to accident.* The gardener's death was ruled *undetermined*, his body interred near the tool shed where he lived. Joan Louise lies in the estate's mausoleum, which she shares uneasily with her parents.

Winds continue to blow strong through the overgrown gardens of the Sanders' estate. To this day, owned by a land trust, the manor house remains vacant, but not unoccupied, on Sweet Water Hill in the hamlet of Crum Creek Run.

Selection published with the author's permission from his most recent work, *Bone Dust*, February, 2022.

Deborah Loughlin
Waldoboro, ME

He Dreams

He Dreams
why the vail goes on
why the vail goes off...
Whispers
Warm smell of sweetness
Blowing gentle wind
Strength of arms and legs
Frames heavy with treasure
Asymmetrical
Symmetrical
Veins feeding wings
Just like dreams of the queen
Dreams of honey
Dreams of bees gone gold

***

Thoughts

My thoughts run rampant
In and out quickly
Closing doors and opening new
I forget where I began
So much to tend to and process
These thoughts are
Fleeting and have changed since ’73
These thoughts, my thoughts have aged and lost their
anger
And gained their mystery and wonder
I have changed in my reasoning—thoughts are hidden deep
But what dethaws gets refrozen

Jeanne Julian
South Portland, ME

To a Student Nearing Commencement

The higher-ups talked of change,
agendas, and reform from
the anchor of the Pier 4 Restaurant podium
while I sat, pink-suited and estranged,
distracted from their hum
by all, windowed behind them,
announcing stasis and momentum:
a crane in suspension, an angled plane,
a duck in lone northward migration
on stubby frantic wings, vigorous
wind edging cold torpor into May again,
a garland of green bridge decorated
with sparkling cars, the progression
of tugs unfurling surf atop the scum
of rumpled, tarnished water trying
to take direction from the rushing clouds
but, within the harbor's frame,
never learning the ocean's range.

And you. On the verge of entrance
into the shiny pinwheels of revolving doors,
the conga of skyscrapers.
Or the drift of continents.

Phillip L. Radoff
Wayland, MA

Butterflies

"Daddy, quick, it's moving, the caterpillar's moving! We have to let it out." The words came out in a torrent of excitement and concern, as six-year-old Jeffrey tugged on his father's sleeve and urged him out of the comfort of a lazy afternoon in late spring to the bedroom that Jeffrey shared with Michael, his three-year-old brother.

Having succeeded in coaxing his father into the bedroom, Jeffrey pointed excitedly to a set of shelves hung on the wall between the twin beds. On either side of the central shelf (high enough to avoid catastrophe, low enough to be seen by a six-year-old standing atop a set of portable steps) were identical pickle jars, each containing: one twig, one clump of leaves (small), and one cocoon (previously motionless).

The jars' contents had been collected the previous fall on a Sunday afternoon with a touch of frost in the air, an early portent of an unusually harsh winter. The boys' mother had roused the rest of the family from mid-weekend idleness to enjoy the fine weather by going for a walk in the woods. Not the deep woods, of course—just a well-traveled footpath by the side of a creek in the nearby state park. So, after lunch, they had all driven the few miles to the park and started along their way.

"I'm going to find a caterpillar and take it home and watch it turn into a butterfly," Jeffrey announced. His parents smiled knowingly and silently congratulated each other on their modest investment in the butterfly book presented to Jeffrey on his recent birthday.

As the family started along the path, Jeffrey bolted off to examine a nearby stand of aspens. Michael let go of his mother's hand and hastened to pursue his brother. With Michael close at his heels like a new puppy, Jeffrey ran from tree to tree, stopping only long enough to inspect the nearest

Phillip L. Radoff
Wayland, MA

branches before bounding off to a more promising prospect. The boys' parents made more leisurely progress along the path and kept a watchful eye on the boys at the approach of the occasional afternoon jogger and odd cyclist.

They had not gone far when Jeffrey called out triumphantly, "Here's one—and look! There's another one, just like the picture in my butterfly book." His father dutifully stooped to inspect two rather drab green caterpillars, camouflaged by the leaves they were slowly munching. "Let's take them home...can we?" Jeffrey asked. "One for me and one for Michael."

"They're not very pretty," said his mother.

"My caterpillar book says those are the best kind," asserted Jeffrey.

His parents exchanged glances. "Sure, take them home," said his mother, "but let's finish our walk first. They'll still be here when we come back."

Jeffrey protested. "But what if somebody else finds them before we come back?"

"Highly unlikely," said his father.

"Anyway," said his mother, "there are plenty of other fish in the sea."

"What do fish have to do with it?" asked Jeffrey plaintively, accompanying his parents and brother with a distinct lack of enthusiasm.

At last they turned back, and Jeffrey ran on ahead to defend his caterpillars against any later claimants. While he stood guard, his father returned to the car for a small cardboard box and a pocket-knife. Carefully severing the sections of leafy branch on which the caterpillars were munching, the boys' father trimmed away the excess foliage so that only two six-inch segments remained, each supporting a motionless caterpillar, oblivious to the imminent changes in its environment. The branches and a few additional leaves were entrusted to Jeffrey, who positioned them with great care in the box and slowly made his way back to the car, where he pressed the box tightly against his chest to protect it against the vagaries of his father's driving.

The large pickle jars had been the boys' mother's contribution. "We'd better wash them first," she had said; "I don't think pickle juice is caterpillars' food of choice." Jeffrey himself had made the transfer of the caterpillar-laden branches from the cardboard box to the now sterilized pickle jars. His father had poked a few air holes in each lid and affixed a square of masking tape to each jar for ready identification of each boy's treasure. "Now," Jeffrey said, "we just have to wait."

And waited they had. Initially the pickle jars had been placed in an out-of-the-way corner of the family's unheated garage so that the caterpillars could winter over. As fall gave way to winter, the caterpillars had consumed most of the leaves and formed cocoons, suspended from the upper portions of the branches.

Throughout the long winter the cocoons had remained motionless and unchanging. When the first crocuses appeared, the boys' father had retrieved the pickle jars from the garage and positioned them on the shelf in the bedroom...and the boys had waited. Mornings after waking, afternoons upon returning from school, evenings before dinner, and nights at bedtime Jeffrey would carefully remove his jar (the one with the letter "J" on the masking tape), place it on his desk, and holding his breath, inspect the cocoon through his magnifying glass, looking in vain for the first faint stirrings that the butterfly book had assured him would come. Only mildly disappointed, he would replace his jar and take down Michael's (the one with "M" on the masking tape) for a more perfunctory look, while Michael stood by, smiling as always but still silent at age three. Again, nothing.

And so Jeffrey would replace Michael's jar and go on about the business of sleeping and eating, attending school and doing homework, until it was again time for cocoon

Phillip L. Radoff
Wayland, MA

inspection.

Michael was present for each inspection. Jeffrey made it a point to summon him from whatever important three-year-old activities he was engaged in, and Michael readily accompanied his older brother to the inspection site. "Okay, kid," Jeffrey would say, the big brother in him instinctively asserting itself, "it's time to check the cocoons. Pretty soon the butterflies will come out, and then we have to open the jars so they won't bang their wings and die."

But Michael would just smile, sometimes giggle a little and nod without speaking, his unvarying response to all overtures from his brother as well as his parents and others. "He'll speak when he's ready," his grandmother had said at first. Then, "Maybe you should take him to a specialist," as he passed his second birthday in silence. And so they had. Pediatricians, speech therapists, ear-nose-and-throat doctors, a psychologist.

"He laughs when you tickle him, and his vocal chords look okay," said the pediatrician.

"There doesn't seem to be any organically causative factor," said the specialists.

"Except for his lack of verbal communication, his cognitive responses are normal," said the psychologist.

"Maybe he's just not ready," they all said, echoing the grandmother.

"But does he understand what we say to him?" his parents wanted to know.

"Sure he does," said Jeffrey, who seemed to take Michael's silence for granted. So the family waited.

Michael and Jeffrey also waited and continued to inspect the pickle jars four times each day without fail, Michael smiling and happy, Jeffrey impatient but still hopeful. A bright child, Jeffrey had recited nursery rhymes at Michael's age, taught himself to read at four, and begun to take an interest in insects at five, to the amusement of his father, the acquiescence of his mother, and the utter disgust of his grand-

Phillip L. Radoff
Wayland, MA

mother. "I will not stay in a house with spiders," she had exclaimed on the first of her visits following the initial appearance of spiders in her grandson's fishbowl.

So during Grandmother's visits they farmed out the spider colony to the keeping of neighbors, who accorded it a loyal if unenthusiastic acceptance and relinquished it willingly at the end of each grandmotherly visit, to be placed once again on the shelf in the boys' bedroom.

It was the very shelf that now held the pickle jar marked with the "J" in which life had begun to reassert itself between breakfast and mid-afternoon on this fine day in late spring.

"All right, let's see now," said Jeffrey's father, after walking at glacial pace (so it seemed) into the bedroom. He peered through the magnifying glass for several seconds, watched with impatience by Jeffrey. They were soon joined by Michael and his mother, who had heard Jeffrey's shouts and now, lured away from their own less consequential afternoon pursuits, looked on with curiosity. "Is it really moving?" asked the boys' mother. "Sure it is," her son replied, "isn't it, Dad?"

"Well . . . yes, it is! The cocoon is breaking open and I can see something coming out! Let's get it outside." He hastened to remove the lids of both pickle jars and set them carefully on the floor.

"Can I carry it, Dad?" asked Jeffrey. "Okay," replied his father. "Just be careful and don't run. There's plenty of time before it hatches completely."

They went out to the yard in slow and careful procession, Jeffrey with his pickle jar in front of him held firmly with both hands, closely followed by his father and less closely by his mother. Michael remained in the house with his own pickle jar.

The family's backyard was alive with the colors and sounds of spring. Bees visited the pansies and daffodils while a family of jays flew back and forth among the trees to no apparent purpose. Oblivious to all but his pickle jar, Jeffrey selected a shady spot on the patio and lowered his burden.

Phillip L. Radoff
Wayland, MA

The cocoon continued to rupture as the creature within struggled to complete its extraordinary transformation from insignificant worm to winged magnificence. The three human creatures, products of less dramatic transformations, looked on silently as the process unfolded.

"Here it comes," Jeffrey whispered, and indeed it did, a splendid swallowtail butterfly, its yellow and black wings fluttering rapidly as it struggled to pull away from its former home and prison. After a few panicked attempts to fly through the walls of the pickle jar, the butterfly soon found its way to the mouth of the jar, and then up it soared and away to freedom.

They watched with pleasure and an odd sense of pride as the small creature flew erratically higher until it was almost out of sight. But as the adults began to turn away, their son cried out in panic. "No!" Jeffrey screamed. "No, no, get away, get away!" With increasing frustration and anxiety the three humans watched helplessly as one of the larger jays detached itself from the branch on which it had perched and advanced toward the swallowtail. Lazily, without effort it seemed, the jay moved unerringly toward the newborn creature while Jeffrey screamed his warning from below.

To no avail. The bird's beak closed around the butterfly and dispatched it in one gulp. The beautiful creature, so carefully nurtured and finally set loose in triumph, was gone in a matter of seconds.

Jeffrey exploded in an outburst of frustration, rage, and...profanity. He shouted at the top of his lungs, and then dissolved in tears. But the jay took no notice as it returned to its branch, there, perhaps, to consider its next meal.

Jeffrey's parents, however, stood in shock. Never before had they heard their son use such language. They themselves had scrupulously avoided profanity in the children's presence, and in the innocence of early parenthood, had assumed that six-year-olds would not yet have been exposed to the language of the streets, much less have learned to dis-

Phillip L. Radoff
Wayland, MA

play such an uninhibited fluency in their presence.

They hesitated, uncertain, looking now at each other, now at their son, whose cries of rage had given way to sobs. Instinctively, they moved closer to him, as if by their proximity to cushion him against the shock of nature's reality and themselves against the loss of the innocence that his spontaneous and unabashed profanity had destroyed.

Then in the silence between sobs came a new sound—a small, unfamiliar, yet unmistakable and wonderful voice. "Bi'fly," said Michael. And as the parents turned toward their younger son, grief struggling with amazement, they heard again, "Bi'fly! See, Daddy? Mommy? Bi'fly."

The happy child, no longer silent, had been forgotten by the others in the excitement of the birth of Jeffrey's butterfly and the horror of its abrupt end. Michael had carried his own pickle jar to the yard, and it now rested on the ground. Now Michael was pointing excitedly upward, and as they followed his gaze they saw another magnificent swallowtail butterfly, black and gold against the sparkling blue of the cloudless spring afternoon. Away it flew in a slow, spiral ascent, away from the pickle jar and the small pointing figure, away from the house and out of sight of the jays. It continued its climb to the temporary safety of the thicket of trees rimming the nearby woods, there to encounter a fate that the humans below could only guess at, but for which they could no longer hold themselves accountable.

But the parents now had little interest in the swallowtail; they had seen many butterflies in their time. They stood silently, not wishing to risk interrupting the first rush of words ever uttered by their young son. "Look, Je'fwy," he called again, "bi'fly."

Jeffrey wiped away his tears and moved to his brother's side, not the least surprised to hear Michael's voice. "Yeah, Michael," he said, placing his arm around his brother's shoulders, "I told you. I told you it would turn into a butterfly."

Rebecca Brooks
Topsham, ME

Where the River Bends

Flowering crab apples
pull on their arched branches
as they settle a breath from the ground.
The limbs do not surrender
despite a remarkable weight.
A resolve that marvels the strongest oak,
who lost a bough this winter.

Shy fiddleheads,
congregating at the river's edge,
begin to unfurl for Spring.
A mother raccoon visits
and patiently teaches her curious cubs
how to wash their breakfast.

Across the turbulent rapids
in a quiet clearing,
the fawn lies motionless.
Only the slight twitch of a nose
proves her existence.
She sleeps in a bed
of dandelion fluff and clover.
This perfect disguise and calm instinct
ensures her survival
from any who travel through the vale.

Rebecca Brooks
Topsham, ME

A faction of weeping willows and quaking aspen
keep the river waters cool,
as their arms hover above the swells.
Thankful they grace his banks,
he knows they can survive his seasonal flood
and provide food and shelter
for the biome natives.
He enjoys the willow's occasional caress
as a zephyr fans her catkins.

The life he supports
allows him contentment
as he encounters each hushed hoofbeat
and tender paw.
With the melodies of countless fowl
and the scent of untold flora,
his pulse is felt at every turn.

***

Julie Babb
Damariscotta, ME

Masked

The roses did not bloom for me this summer.
Perhaps they were too busy
Polishing their fervent green leaves,
Or perhaps they simply forgot...
I went to them, asking why
And they answered, "But we did!
Red, yellow, pink and white!"
Then I saw—and realized
It was I who did not bloom this summer.

Jean Biegun
Davis, CA

Winter Wish

Winter, and the trees
hold tightly to the ground.

My first time perceiving
that steadfast union,
new honor stirred:

the reaching roots,
the substantial ready soil,
their pact, their dance,
their fruitful anchored bond.

And born from that joining
come every bursting nest,
abundant orchard summers,
autumn's stored seed.

Remembering deer cooling in shade,
an owl dozing in a hollow trunk,
and woodpeckers mining grubs,
an elemental child-like wish
begins to grow:

Tree holding ground,
ground holding tree,
may something that matters
hold tight to me.

R. Craig Lord
Cushing, ME

Mudflats

She washed the glass and the plate. Careful not to slip. The plate with the blueberry pattern had been her mom's. Mom had lived twenty years by herself. She placed them in the drying rack. No need to run the dishwasher. She gazed out the window to the harbor below. The setting sun had turned the sky into a mixture of pinks and purples. The incoming tide carried with it the smell of pines and salt. A lone mooring ball bobbed up and down.

"Tide's changing, Paul. Looks like the wind is picking up. I hope you checked that mooring line."

"Ah sweetie, thanks for being concerned, but I think she'll hold."

"Remember when Finnerty's boat got loose. I looked up and there she was headed for the mud. No one in sight."

"I remember that too. It was all hands on deck. We both got a little muddy that night."

"We took our clothes off in the dooryard. I nearly froze to death."

"Turned out to be a pretty great night, as I remember it."

"One of our best nights, dear. Wrapped in a blanket by the fire. You were always there to keep me warm."

"The pleasure was mine. Forty years with you. Who could ask for more?"

"I do. I do every day. Anyhow tonight I am going to finish with your clothes."

"Not going to watch the Sox? You love the Sox. The clothes can wait."

"I like the Sox because you liked the Sox. If I don't fold your clothes they never will get folded."

"Ah, watch the Sox. It will be like old times. And turn up the heat, it's cold in here."

"It's your rule, Paul. The heat doesn't go on until October

R. Craig Lord
Cushing, ME

15th."

"C'mon, Marie, splurge a little. I want you to be happy."

"You made me very happy. Very happy. But things still have to get done. I'm going to fold those clothes."

"Okay, but leave the game on. You can come down and watch it when you're finished."

"I will, but I'll never be finished."

***

Stacie Santillo
York, PA

Porcelain

I was not born into wealth my silver spoon—plated
my privilege—a safety pin I used to weave
among the elastic of my hand-me-down panties
where thread once held them tight against
my sisters' bellies.

Growing up, humble was my currency, it wasn't
worth much then, wouldn't buy anything
in those days, but I held on to it and deposited it
into a bank shaped like character.

Every year, my grandmother filled that bank
with her perseverance and resolve. I still remember
the sound of her voice as it plinked against the
porcelain edges of my heart.

Jeffery M. Bishop, Sr.
Freedom, ME

Fragile Strength

A fragile thing that possesses a strength immeasurable
Kept in reserve deep down
Nurtured and guarded with all the vigilance of a parent to
their child
Its meaning known only to the one who sustains it
But understood universally by all who wish to keep their
own alive
In times of strife and misery its light dims almost to
extinction
Yet it's infantile glow sustains life beyond explanation
Living on through the most dire of storms and
circumstance
Such a powerful thing is hope
That we may never remain fallen for its strength will lift us
again

***

Peggy Trojan
Brule, WI

Air Mail

I smile to remember
our eyes meeting
across the room,
your finger casually
brushing your lip,
sending a kiss.

Published in *Talking Stick* 2021

Roselyn Stewart
Brookfield, WI

Storm

The day dawns dark as night.
Puzzled I check my clock.
Yes, 7:30.
I pad into the kitchen on bare
feet and flip the switch on the
coffee maker.
Thunder rumbles in the
Distance.
My kitchen lights reflect in the
darkened glass of the patio doors.
A lightning flash, then thunder
shakes the house. I wait for the
fury of the storm.
Suddenly the trees are still.
I hold my breath. Trees begin
to sway, wind picks up. I pour
myself another cup of coffee
as I wait for rain to splash
against the window panes.
All is quiet. A gentle wind stirs
the trees. Daylight grows stronger.
It becomes obvious all the noise
and commotion was "Much ado
about nothing." I listen to the
radio and sip my coffee.

Scott Carty
Peoria, AZ

Okinawa

What follows are four brief descriptions of surgical procedures that took place on Okinawa in 1974. There were certainly more, but for me, these four best exemplify extraordinary team effort, dedication and care for patients who recover and go home and tears for those who don't.

I was a US Army surgical technician and my job was assisting surgeons during surgery. Passing and holding instruments, wiping the wound with surgical sponges, irrigating the wound, etc. I enjoyed the job and made lifelong friends during my two years on Okinawa.

Case#1

I looked at the schedule for room 2, my room for that day. Our first case was a removal of a piece of shrapnel from a Vietnam vet who was leaving the Army to resume private life with his wife and two kids with another one on the way. He had been wounded years earlier in his left ankle and decided to have the shrapnel removed before he left the service. The surgery was routine. It took us about ten minutes to find the shrapnel and remove it. The surgeon closed the wound and sent the patient off to the recovery room. Enjoy private life; you've earned it. Two days later I received a call from the floor that this same patient was spiking a fever of 104 and was semi-conscious. Doctors on the floor and nursing staff were unable to find anything that would cause these symptoms. The decision was made to do an exploratory laparotomy (open the abdomen), to see if they could find anything that was causing his temperature to rise so suddenly and to such a high level.

I called in the crew and we set up the room. It was about 11:30 PM. While we were setting up the room, the patient was just outside the door on a gurney. I stopped and asked if he needed anything. He was about 6'6" and had huge hands. He was shaking and said he was cold. I put another warm blanket on the three he already had.

He grabbed my hand and said, "Doc, I'm really scared, what's wrong with me?" (In our surgical garb, we all looked the same.)

I replied, "We're all professionals, we're experts, we know what we're doing and we're going to fix what's making you sick."

He said, "Thanks, Doc," and closed his eyes. I gave his hand a reassuring squeeze and went about my work.

After the patient was asleep, the surgeon opened up his abdomen and we started looking for anything that could create his symptoms. We were looking for an appendix or bowel problem or anything else that would cause such a dramatic temperature rise. Everyone was getting anxious and frustrated at not finding the source of his problem. About 30 minutes into the case the anesthesiologist suddenly said, "I'm losing this guy, I can't keep his pressure up."

We had two units of blood and IVs going in and he was hooked up to all the necessary equipment. We even had him on a cooling pad to help keep his temperature down. The surgeon said, "I haven't found a damn thing that would cause this, let's close him up and get him to ICU STAT." We did a quick temporary closure using huge needles and made just enough stitches to keep his belly closed. I called ICU and told them to send a bed to surgery and expect a critical patient in five minutes. The room looked like Keystone Kops. The anesthesiologist was barking instructions to everyone while the surgeon was still trying to finish closing the guy. Finally, we used sterile sponges to pack the incision site as best we could. I went outside the room and brought in the bed that ICU had just delivered. We lifted him onto the bed and transferred all the IVs and equipment to the new bed. We lifted the side rails and pushed the bed out of the OR toward the main door of the surgery department.

Scott Carty
Peoria, AZ

The anesthesiologist was at the head of the bed with an ambu bag squeezing air into his lungs, since he was still intubated and paralyzed from the anesthesia. There was a doctor on either side of him and I was at the foot of the bed. The head of the bed went through the door and then stuck in the door frame. We pushed for all we were worth and it only made the bed tighter. The anesthesiologist and surgeon were going ballistic, cursing and screaming about this damn bed. I finally ran from that door to a side door and joined the anesthesiologist at the head of the bed. On the count of three we all pulled and pushed as hard as we could and suddenly the door jam busted loose from the wall and the bed broke free. There was wood and plaster and dust everywhere. ICU was at the far end of the hallway. We sprinted with the bed to ICU. About halfway down the hallway we passed his wife who was holding their two children. She had seen the entire incident and her eyes were as big as silver dollars and she had this look of horror on her face which I shall never forget...

We got the patient hooked up to all the equipment in ICU and slowly walked back to surgery. We were all emotionally and physically drained, soaking wet from sweat, no one spoke. We slowly cleaned and restocked the room for the morning's cases. It was about 2:30 in the morning when we finally finished; we went to the coffee room and collapsed onto whatever furniture was available. The surgeon finally came back from ICU with tears in his eyes. "He's gone," he said and started to cry. We all hugged and started crying as well. It was an emotional, heartbreaking, moment.

We had all been in cases where the patient didn't make it (surgery was their last chance) and you feel sad for the family and quickly question, "Did we do anything that caused it?" Then you move on. This one was different. This one was going to be with us for a long time. (It's been nearly 50 years and I still get a lump in my throat.) I still see his wife, looking at us in horror thinking, I'm sure, we were at least partially

Scott Carty
Peoria, AZ

responsible for her husband's death.

The autopsy found nothing that would have caused his death. In the end, there was no closure for his family or for us. Occasionally, I still wonder if it was something we did or didn't do that caused his untimely death. Someone suggested there may have been a sort of toxin encapsulated in the shrapnel, that had remained dormant until we removed it from his ankle. I like to think it was something like that if for no other reason then to provide a cause.

The next day, we were the talk of the entire surgery department with our door busting antics. It was so simple: with the side rails up, the bed was two inches wider than with them down. Of course if we had thought it through, we would have realized that was the problem and lowered them to get through the door; but with all hell breaking loose, we weren't thinking very clearly. Another factor was that the ICU bed was a "real" hospital bed, rather than a surgery gurney and so was wider to begin with. What I found interesting was that the individual doors to each operating room were wide enough even with the bed rails up, but the main door into the entire surgical suite was not wide enough. Go figure! By the way, since we had done the demolition for them, they decided to widen the door so that would never happen again.

A mandatory review of the case was required since the patient died following surgery. Numerous factors were looked at and dismissed. No one was at fault or blamed for anything done before or after the case.

We never talked about that case again. It was too painful and brought up tortuous questions we had no answers for. I hope his wife and children were able to move on with their lives. Me? I rarely think about it. Too painful to feel his hand squeezing mine, to see her eyes looking at us in horror, and all the "what ifs?" can drive you crazy. Sometimes, I just simply tell him: "We tried buddy, we really tried!"

Scott Carty
Peoria, AZ

Case #2

It was my turn to take call, which meant we stayed in the hospital, in the surgery suit in case there was an emergency. It was probably after midnight when I got a call from Labor and Delivery, and a frantic nurse yelled into the phone, "Dr. Smith is doing a C-section (Cesarean-Section), in five minutes with or without anesthesia."

I quickly scanned the list of anesthesiologists and found who was on call that evening and gave him a call. When he picked up the phone I said, "Dr. Smith is doing a C-section in five minutes with or without you." (He only lived two blocks from the hospital and took off in a dead run still in his pajamas.)

I quickly ran up the two flights of stairs to L&D. We keep a C-Section instrument tray already made up and sterile exactly for this type of situation so I was ready to go in less than two minutes. I held the knife in my hand ready to give to the surgeon who was yelling, "Give me the knife, give me the knife."

The patient was still awake and her eyes were as big as saucers. I thought, *Why are you still awake*? It was then that I noticed another doctor was standing between her legs and was covered in blood and other bodily fluids pushing for all he was worth a small head protruding from her uterus. He was trying to push the infant back into the uterus It was also very obvious why they were pushing the baby back. The umbilical cord was wrapped tightly around his neck and every involuntary push the mother made, tightened the strangle hold on the infant's neck.

I was just about to hand the surgeon the knife when the anesthesiologist burst into the room, saw the situation, grabbed a syringe from his "go" bag and said, "Give me 30 seconds" as he emptied the contents of the syringing into the tube taped to her wrist. "Go," he said and the surgeon wasted no time slicing his way to the uterus. What would normally take about 20 minutes, he accomplished in less than

30 seconds. Once inside the uterus he felt for the umbilical cord and pulled it gently but firmly until the other doctor felt the tug. It was quite a scene—one doctor pulling the umbilical cord out of the incision while the other doctor pushed the baby back into the uterus. Within a few minutes the baby was back in the uterus and was delivered in a "normal" C-Section procedure. He was handed off to the pediatrician and quickly examined for any signs of trauma or oxygen starvation. The baby was just fine. The poor doctor who had been pushing the baby back was completely exhausted and his arms were almost to the point of spasms. He was sore for almost a week. The mother suffered no long term effects, with the exception of a longer incision scar; the baby was completely healthy and did just fine. We reviewed the case and determined that "we" the surgery department, had followed the book. Which is another way of saying, "Scott, you did good, but then there's always room for improvement."

Case #3

About 6:30 in the evening, I received a call from the emergency room that an ambulance was on its way from the air base located about eight miles away. A 21-year-old airman had accidentally flipped his jeep and hit his head on a rock. The neurosurgeon was already on his way to the hospital. I quickly called in the rest of the staff and prepared Rm1 for the case. When he arrived in surgery his eyes were swollen shut, his vitals were dangerously low and he actually appeared lifeless. What usually takes about 10–15 minutes in preparing the patient for surgery we did in one minute—ignoring all the safety protocols and double checks that were standard procedure, as it was obvious this patient didn't have 15 minutes to spare. The anesthesiologistt did a crash intubation as the surgeon shaved his entire head. Once shaved, we placed his head in a torture-looking device that has three very sharp points that actually pierce the skin and come in contact with his skull. It is then tightened and secured so there is absolutely no way the head can move. This is obviously critical when working in someone's brain. The surgeon took an air-driven saw and cut away the bone over the area that was damaged in the fall. He said, "Place a bucket under his head, when I lift this flap. He will either bleed out and die or not."

I placed the bucket under his head and stood back. The surgeon stood to one side and lifted the flap, suddenly a thin jet stream of blood under tremendous pressure, shot up and hit the ceiling. I thought, *This guy's dead*, and looked at the surgeon.

He said, "I think we can save this guy." He quickly grabbed a staple gun-like instrument and placed two staples on the tiny hole. The bleeding stopped. Wow! The surgeon explained that the dura is a very thin but very strong lining surrounding the brain, similar to wax paper. It works great until there is a tear and then it simply rips apart. Since there was just a small hole in the dura, it didn't have a chance to split. If it had been any bigger, the pressure would have ripped it apart and he would have bled out in less than a minute with us helpless to stop it.

A few days later, I saw the patient in the cafeteria with his parents. The Air Force flew them direct to Okinawa free of charge the same day he was injured and presumed DOA-(Dead on Arrival). His head was wrapped in surgical dressings, his eyes were black and blue, and his color was a little off, but he was alive and talking as if nothing had happened. I thought to myself, *Kid you have no idea how close you came.*

Case # 4

A marine was injured in a bar fight on a Friday night and had to call his own ambulance. He was bleeding from a gash in his neck from a broken beer bottle. His jugular vein was severed and he would bleed out in a few minutes without pressure being applied to the wound. When he arrived at the

Scott Carty
Peoria, AZ

hospital he was shipped directly to surgery where we quickly put him under and started to work. The surgeon said, "I want four units of blood stat. What's his blood type?" No one knew as he was now unconscious and no one had thought to ask him. His dog tags were gone and presumed to still be in the bar. "Well how the hell can we give him blood if we don't know his type?" No one spoke. Doesn't matter, give him four units of type 0." (The universal type.)

We called down to the lab and told them we needed four units of type 0. The lab replied back, "We don't have four units of 0, only one."

This information was relayed to the surgeon and he went ballistic. "I want four units of type 0 and I want it yesterday." The tech in the lab was getting understandably frustrated, it was not his fault; he was just relaying the facts.

The anesthesiologist said, "Call AFRTS (Armed Forces Radio and TV Station), and say there is an emergency need for blood at the hospital."

This was relayed to the tech. "I can't do that, we'll have people all over the place and I'm the only one here."

The surgeon replied, "I don't care if we get 100 guys out there, I want that blood now!"

A few minutes later, an emergency signal went over the AFRTS airways, "There is an emergency need for blood at the hospital, please donate ASAP." The tech had called his boss and all available techs were called in for the emergency blood draws. We were thinking maybe 20 or 30 Marines, soldiers, and Airman would show up. Within 20 minutes there were almost 100 service men and women in a line that went out the lab through the hallway and into the night. Each service was betting the other services that they had more donors than the others; money was collected and held for the final talley. More arrived. The banter and joke telling was non-stop. A portable radio was playing outside. The lab ran out of blood donor bags and called other military and civilian hospitals, clinics, etc., to send over their extras. It was a zoo.

Scott Carty
Peoria, AZ

But amid the chaos, it seemed to dawn on all of us I thought, *We may be a different service, color, sex, etc., but it didn't matter. We were all united in helping to save the life of a fellow serviceman.*

The surgeon got the blood he needed, the surgery was a success, the lab processed blood well into the early morning, shipping blood to other hospitals and clinics and if I remember right, the Marines won the final count with the other services close to a tie.

I still get teary-eyed when I think back on that case and how we came together to help one in need and indeed others unseen and unknown. I felt privileged to be a small part of it.

***

Grace B. Sheridan
Cutler, ME

Cosmos

The cosmos went tall this summer:
tall enough in the frequent rain
to fill the double-hung window
above the mid-line sash with fernery
and blossoms in my line of vision
as I savor sautéed chicken, rice and greens
served with honey mustard dressing
in a white ceramic bowl and bees flit
stamen to stamen, sip to sip, feasting
from swaying fuschia-petaled plates,
on the nectar of a gallery piece
Cosmos in October Breeze.

Karen E. Wagner
Hudson, MA

Snow Melt

These aren't the days
of my youth when winter
came and stayed awhile.
Now I wait long for you
to flock the fields,
picture the scene
inside a glass globe.

Snowshoes stashed
in the clutter of the garage,
expect a run through
fresh trails. I agree.
Creatures of the gray morn
have left their prints
there before me.
Little matter,
their feet are small.

I give all of me to this season.
I miss the shade
of summer
that could keep the snow.
And the colored leaves
of autumn that hold
the stained glass patterns
of late frost, then comes fluffed snow.

Perhaps I should move north.
Paint me like the arctic fox.
Winter comes, find me there.
Amid the drifts
and ice-bound thistles.

Karen E. Wagner
Hudson, MA

I focus on what I have,
rather than not.
One day of snow,
a month of cold dark and black ice.
Three months till spring,
more than half past the solstice.
I've placed me
in the scheme of time.
I melt quickly like the snow.

***

Brandon Ying Kit Boey
Falmouth, ME

The Leaf Blower

You stand as a small silhouette
Watching while the cold leaves whir
Your head peaked in a hat
Hands in gloves holding your spade
As I move forward, I turn to see you balancing
on the cord
I wave with my hand and as I do the machine
roars your direction
And you jump and prance away
In a trail of shrieks
I turn back and feel your squeals farther now,
by the house, on the rocks, skipping across the
dark
As now the light retreats
While the leaves fleet in the whirlwind
Driven to bare the ground
And I going after them,
You see me fade into the wood.

Judith Grey
Nobleboro, ME

Ice-in on the Great Salt Bay

Ice slabs rise and fall unhinged on the tide.
Like a loon whose runway is freezing up,
I circle my own territory, recalculate,

break from the grip of winter funk. Outside
wind chill tightens my bare patch face
sun-struck under saturated blue.

At cove's edge, green water chops,
stretches kintsugi hairline weakness
above the groan and suck.

Gumdrop smelt shacks at the head of the bay.
Underfoot, brittle tide wash ice,
perfect skimmers for tossing.

Ah, the delicate Siren sounds:
whoosh, slink, brush, phshoooooossshh.
The cove glitters in crystal fragment bling,

hums on the fault lines of ice shrug.
I step out onto the hardened bay
inches above a foreign place

where rainbow smelts run on the tide,
dodge predator fish, circle jig lines
dangling silver, heavy with free lunch bait.

What do smelts know of hooks,
and who hasn't taken a chance on thin ice,
given in to the urgency of shine,

Judith Grey
Nobleboro, ME

the offer
of both delight and oblivion
on the same disinterested plane.

***

Janet Dorman
Falmouth, ME

Black Box

A plane goes down, no one knows why.
Turbulence undetected, birds in the engine?
"We will know once we find the black box,"
the official says. "And we will find it."

The black box knows all,
holds all secrets and mysteries,
keeps them safe under hundreds of feet of water.
Answers will be found.

I stare at a black box sitting atop
the butcher block that you helped to
haul out of storage some years back.
A useless bit of antiquary, taking up space.

This black box, too, holds secrets and mysteries,
but it will keep them, even upon opening.
They will scatter with the ash that flies from my hand
to drift up and out and down to earth and rock

And to the surface of the water
where you swam last summer,
sinking slowly, taking with them
the answers for your absence.

E. M. Barsalou
East Kingston, NH

Wooden Plank Trail

Out past the towns and city limits
There is a place that I love to empower.
A reason for leaving is the reason
I'm breathing; a nurtured endeavor for the life I've been
missing.
Out past the fields and a low banked river,
The forests arise like a fairytale ritual;
Everything encompassed and set for a destination.
A beautiful place where you can put your thoughts
together,
Down an old path that leads to a meadow.
A familiar smell and sight which encumbers the
Well spring of life with the longness of winter gets closer to
your soul.
A lot like Autumn or Spring, it's memory of
Your childhood, it will not ever fail.
Once you've taken it back and you soon remember
How you found and told yourself
Where to find the wooden plank trail down below
The river is where you'll be found in its embrace...

***

Sylvia Little-Sweat
Wingate, NC

Woodland Time

Morning—fresh deer tracks,
Noon—scampering squirrels at play,
Night—owl lullabies.

Elizabeth Lombardo
Walpole, ME

The Exchange

They met at McDonald's and ordered separately. There could be no thoughts of owing favors. The mother and child went first: a cheeseburger Happy Meal and a Big Mac with Coke. The man: just a coffee, no cream. When the brown tray was handed over the counter, they took their food and sat down in a booth. The child looked expectantly from his cheeseburger to his mother.

"Will you say grace?" she asked distractedly, plunging a straw into the sweaty cup of cola. From the other side of the booth, the man silently removed his baseball cap and folded his hands over it. The child began to pray over his french fries.

"Bless us oh Lord, and these, Thy gifts..."

At the "amen," his little bowed head popped up, eyes widening as they caught sight of the toy spaceship peeking out between the fries inside the bag. Conversation was sparse as one side of the booth devoured its burgers. Between sips of coffee, the man attempted to dig up innocuous memories to steady the mood. Finding nothing to preserve his balance on the strained tightrope of this meeting, he resigned himself to cursing the heat in these parts. The mother laughed knowingly and told him to stay in the air conditioned dining room while she went out for a smoke.

With the mother gone, the man felt more at ease. He knew what to say to the child, who, for his part, had taken little notice of his mother's absence. The man grabbed the toy spaceship and removed the plastic that kept the greasy fries from getting all over it. "Look," he showed the child. "The alien fries are attacking the ship! Quick, destroy them!" The child's ketchup-covered face formed a smile as he crammed the last few fries into his mouth.

When the mother returned from her cigarette, the child

Elizabeth Lombardo
Walpole, ME

was finished eating. "Can I go and play now?" he asked. The party relocated to the playroom adjacent to the dining room. The man immediately missed the air conditioning in this room. The sticky air was mingled with the scent of even stickier plastic. The mother and child didn't seem to notice.

After removing his flip flops, the child entered the bright red maze of tubes and nets and slides. The grown-ups sat down to watch the child. The bench where they sat was sticky, too.

The man could feel himself being bonded to the cracked blue vinyl by someone's spilled soda. Unable to look at the other, the man and the mother shifted uncomfortably. She busied herself with her phone until the child's pleas for attention were too loud to ignore. The weight of missed years fell on the shoulders of the man as he looked up to watch the child play. It conspired with the heat to suffocate him where he sat. The child giggled as he jumped into a ball pit, but his mother's eyes had already returned to her phone. The man applauded the child, but he was already too busy diving into the multi-colored plastic to notice. The man's gaze wandered to the window. The traffic outside passed by the glass-encased playroom, marking seconds, minutes; it was impossible to tell how long the adults allowed the silence to build. Suddenly, the mother spoke.

"So, what do you want to know?"

"I don't know. Start at the beginning, I guess."

Marilyn Weymouth Seguin
Akron, OH

Where Jerzee Lies

Will you get another dog, they ask.
It has only been a week since Jerzee died.
Just today I removed the blanket from the end of my bed
That marked the place where Jerzee lies.

It was her time to go, they said.
Her legs were weak and her hips were sore,
Her liver and her kidneys worn.
She slept away most of her days,
Yet when I returned from doing chores,
She greeted me at the door,
With happy barks and dancing tail,
An old dog with a puppy inside.

It has only been a week since Jerzee died.
Come spring I will go to a forest place,
And bury her ashes under the pine
That grows beside the lake.
I will dislodge a stone from the sandy shore,
And with legs weak and hips sore,
I'll carry it to that shady spot
To mark the place where Jerzee lies.

Thomas Fallon
Rumford, ME

Wind from the Sea

Reflection from Andrew Wyeth's
painting ***Wind from the Sea****.*

The curtain blew away
from the window
suddenly
and I saw the road
leading to the sea
and the sky.

The wind stopped.

I stood at the window
looking through
the curtain
to the road and the sea
and the sky

Wind blew the curtain
away from the window
suddenly
and I saw the road and
the sea and
the sky.

The wind stopped.

Olive C. Hart
Newcastle, ME

In the Pea Patch

Day was breaking when I slid quietly from the bed, slipped into old clothes, and tip-toed down the stairs with Kippy at my heels. Through the cool silent house, hoping not to disturb the family, we went to the kitchen, where the aroma of fresh coffee greeted me. I managed to swallow a delicious cupful without burning my tongue while Kippy swiftly emptied her breakfast bowl. I closed the screen door quietly behind us.

Such a perfect July morning in the country! The air was fresh and still night-time cool, smelling green and earthy, a favorite smell. The birds were just waking to herald another clear summer day. One little finch always chose the tallest tip of the spruce tree to serenade the coming sun. Often, if I whistled a few notes to him, he would listen and then sing a sweet answer.

But today no delays; I had to be on my way. Those peas were perfect, ready for picking, and I planned to pick, shell, blanch, and pack them into the freezer before lunch. Well, maybe before dinner. It would depend on how many there were.

I took the path beside the barn, sniffing happily at the meadow fragrance of grasses and flowers. The track was lined on my left with tall grass where spiders seemed to practice their web-building skills. I often saw their webs in the early morning. Ah, there was one today. It was a large one, perfectly shaped, every silky strand pearled with tiny drops of the night-time dew, a real beauty. Suddenly, I wished I had my camera. But no...I had filmed some nice ones on Tuesday. This morning I had paused long enough.

Kippy's warm, furry body against my knee was quivering in her eagerness to keep moving. So, on we went to the garden, where the long green rows of pea vines grew tall and

Olive C. Hart
Newcastle, ME

thick on their wire fencing. After a little of the required sniffing and checking the area, Kippy settled down in the grass at the edge of the garden, her observation post, while I started down the row on the right, picking quickly but carefully to avoid tearing or breaking the vines, leaving them to produce more peas another day. I was amused as usual at the little squeaky noise the pods in my hands made when they rubbed against each other.

At first, the thick green wall of them gave me pause; leaves and pea pods being the same shade of green, so it was hard to distinguish which to pick. But the ripe pods were firm to touch, the leaves soft, and my fingers soon learned the difference, even if I couldn't see them. It was not long before I took a moment to open a pod to sample the sweetness. Delicious right from the vine. Oh, yes, Kippy reminded me that she wanted a turn, too. I opened her pod, and she was quick to come down the row. Then she carried it back to her grassy spot where she settled down to pick the peas out with her teeth. Yum, yum.

The silence surrounded me as if I were the only person in the world. The one sound was the buzzing of the honeybees, bumbling contentedly among the sweet blossoms farther up the vine above me, collecting the sugary treasure for delivery to their queen.

A cow mooed from the dairy farm up the road. Must be milking time. Later a screen door slapped shut and a car started down the road—our neighbor on the way to work the early shift. By now I had finished my row, turned, and started back up the other side.

The sun had risen and was warming my back. The basket was getting heavy, and I picked on. Time for Kippy's second treat. Two was her limit because her tummy was a little finicky if we strayed far from her regular dog food diet.

It became warmer and warmer down between the rows of vines, and I was glad to hear a small voice calling.

"Mummy, there you are. Are you gonna come cook break-

Olive C. Hart
Newcastle, ME

fast?"

"Yes, I'll come right now, okay?"

"Yeah, did you pick all the peas?"

"No, but I'll leave the rest for our supper. What do you want for breakfast?"

"Pancakes. Blueberry pancakes. They're the best."

"Sounds good. I think I can do that."

We took the homeward path, the heavy basket in my right hand, Julie's small hand in my left, and Kippy leading the way. Before I stepped inside the back door, I paused for one more deep breath of fresh air, a glance at the clear blue of the sky, the rich green of grass, old-fashioned pink roses hanging over the old stone wall, and the trumpet vine climbing over the kitchen door. I could hear familiar family sounds inside the house. This might not be heaven, but for me it came pretty close.

***

Peggy Trojan
Brule, WI

Semper Fi

In the last months,
Hospice sent a music therapist
to sing to you.
Knowing your twenty-one-year service,
she sang all three verses
of the "Marine's Hymn."
We saw the tears in your eyes,
watched your spirit stand at attention
and salute

the late Frank J. Lid
Cuyahoga Falls, OH

I Remember

When I look out at the sunset, I remember, and I smile.
Remembering the quiet times with you here at my side,
Sunsets viewed together through brighter, younger eyes
When I look out at the sunset, I remember

When I see some children playing, I remember and I laugh
Remembering the happy times that our little family had.
Playing children we viewed through brighter, younger eyes
When I see the children playing, I remember

When I see sun on the water, I remember and I wink
Remembering the secrets that the two of us had shared
Secrets shared as twinkles in brighter, younger eyes
When I see the sun on the water, I remember

When I view a distant hillside, I remember, and I sigh.
Remembering your arm around me, standing by my side
Viewing toward the future through brighter, younger eyes
When I view the distant hillsides, I remember

When I feel the gentle breezes, I remember, and I cry
Remembering your gentle spirit dancing through my life
A spirit seen forever now through brighter, younger eyes
When I feel the gentle breezes, Dear, I remember you.

Mary Ann Bedwell
Grants, NM

Waiting for the Rain

They call it a "monsoon."
Here in the desert,
But no matter what they call it,
We are still dry.
The roofers say they will finish today,
New gutters wait to deflect the rain into new barrels
When it finally decides to fall.
I look toward the southwest—every afternoon for the past
week
The clouds have formed over the Zuni's,
The skirts of the virga skimming the mountain tops.
Water never touches the ground.

One more day
I will carry water to my garden,
Buckets and buckets to my precious trees,
Taking careful note of what flourishes and what does not,
Planning what to plant next season.

The desert is not my home,
I am a transplant from the lush Midwest,
Slowly mummifying in the arid atmosphere.
Only the rain will save me.

Margaret Roncone
Vashon, WA

On a Cloudy Morning

a lip of blue in the east
promises sun
trees flourishing new leaves
are still in the breezeless air
Raven bawks at the nothingness
of day
what does he know of promise?
My body searching with each footstep
follows the trail of life
the swaying turn of events
shocking our bones

The Sound sparkles like a mine of unearthed diamonds...
crossing this passage how
many times?
A hundred vehicles carried by
a hefty ferry.
Land stretching before our eyes
like a green bristled arm.
Here on this watery place
of travel promise holds tomorrow
like a wet newborn in her arms.

Brenda Smith
Belfast, ME

An Elephant to Remember

Most pre-school children of my generation first became acquainted with the king of the jungle through illustrated storybooks. They fell in love with Babar's frolicking adventures, or Dr. Seuss's famous hero, Horton, who saved Whoville. Not so for me. I first fell in love with an elephant, not a literary one but a real one, right here in Maine. It happened in 1956, in the tiny picturesque seaside community known as Temple Heights.

A few miles along the forested coastline on a rutted dirt road south of the more upscale Bayside village, the summer cottages of Temple Heights clung to the side of a steep hill overlooking Penobscot Bay. Three of my great aunts each owned one of the twenty private cottages dotting the hillside. The centerpiece "Temple" of this spiritualist camp was a windowless square box where believers gathered for spooky séances with the spirits of their departed loved ones.

Great Aunt Adelaide's cottage stood just to the left of the temple on the upper road. Its gambrel shaped roof sheltered a spacious living room with a propane heater, a tiny kitchen, and an even smaller bathroom. A steep narrow staircase led to two unfinished knotty pine bedrooms above. When it rained at night, the drops beat rhythmically on the roof over our heads and the fresh pine scent from the forest outside perfumed the air. A huge deck wrapped around the front and one side of the cottage offering a spectacular view over the bay and beyond to Islesboro.

My younger brother and I could hardly wait to arrive each summer. Quickly donning bathing suits, we scurried down the rutted road, then down a grassy path leading to a weathered lobster shanty perched on an outcrop above the rocky shore. On the shoreline to the right, we collected starfish, sea urchins, shells and strangely shaped driftwood. The water

Brenda Smith
Belfast, ME

was always freezing cold and the seaweed-covered rocks treacherously slippery. At certain times, we had to watch carefully for translucent moon jellyfish drifting in the water. None of that phased us in the least; we loved our fantastical aquatic playground. Only reluctantly, when Mom sternly insisted, would we gather up our new treasures and trudge back up the hill.

As if the ocean's offerings weren't fascinating enough, one afternoon on our way back to the cottage, in the distance, we glimpsed an odd-looking gray creature roughly the size of a small cow clomping toward us. I noticed it had a strange snout that curled and swayed. Coiled around its neck was a thick rope used by a young, dark-skinned stranger to lead the animal. My brother and I were quite curious about this creature. It was stranger than anything we'd ever seen. We stood on the side of the road until they reached us, eager for a closer inspection of this peculiar animal.

The man leading her greeted us. "Meet Kitubinissa. She's friendly and very gentle. You don't need to be afraid. She's just a baby."

"Wow! She's the biggest baby *I've* ever seen," I declared.

The man told us his name was Cyril Ray and that the animal on his lead was an Asian elephant.

I summoned up the courage to touch the elephant's leathery flank, only to find her trunk sweeping around to hover right in front of my face. My brother screeched and fled for his life. I held my ground, torn between awe and terror. Cyril explained they'd walked up the road from the nearby summer estate of Horace Hildreth, a former governor of Maine.

In 1953, the Eisenhower administration appointed Hildreth to be the United States Ambassador to Pakistan. In appreciation of his service, the Pakistani government gifted Hildreth this small elephant as a token of their esteem. Protocol in those days required the acceptance of a gift of this nature. So Kitubinissa traveled halfway around the globe to her new home in Maine, accompanied by Cyril, whose duties included feeding and exercising her.

With my mother's permission, Cyril hoisted me four feet in the air so I could straddle the elephant's shoulders for an unforgettable ride. Kitubinissa followed Cyril as he continued down the road, while I gripped the thick rope around her neck to steady myself as she lumbered along, swaying from side to side with each step. Her towering height, relative to my own, gave me the impression she'd be a giant someday.

Nearly every day after our first introduction, we would see Kitubinissa and Cyril walking up the road to Temple Heights. Cyril told us she loved to chomp on green plants, so as soon as they came into view, I would charge from the cottage down the hill to offer "my" elephant a handful of fresh green grass I snatched from the lawn as I rushed to greet them. The tip of her trunk felt like warm velvet as she swept the gift from my hand. Curling her trunk inward, she stuffed the fresh greens in her mouth. The twinkle in her eyes told me she approved of the treat.

Her strangeness faded and I thought of her as a pet, albeit a rather unique one. She, too, seemed to adjust to the strangeness of her new habitat. At the end of our vacation, we headed home, enriched by the experience of getting to know Kitubinissa. We could hardly wait to tell our playmates that we had made friends with a real elephant. Throughout the winter months, we dreamed of playing with her again on our next vacation.

But by the end of the first summer, she was no longer a baby. The Hildreths decided, when Cyril quit his job as her handler, a zoo would be the best place for her to live and they gifted her to the Stone Zoo in Stoneham, Massachusetts, where she lived until 1990. Ironically, my family lived only ten minutes from the zoo, but I never knew that my dear little elephant lived so close by. One day in the mid-1970's, a few friends and I went on an outing to the small zoo, which despite its proximity, none of us had ever visited.

Brenda Smith
Belfast, ME

Only one elephant lived there. When I read the exhibit signage, it shocked me to discover the Hildreth family had donated this elephant to the zoo. My heart nearly burst with joy. Kitubinissa *had* grown into a magnificent giant!

Excitedly, I told my friends, "I rode on that elephant."

They laughed at my preposterous statement. None of them believed me until I explained I had met her when she was a baby. I watched her for half an hour, wandering in circles around her small dusty enclosure, lonely and bored. This was *not* the fate I had imagined for baby Kitubinissa. She deserved better than to be a captive object of curiosity gawked at by thousands of people.

When I learned later that elephants in the wild lived in herds and were very social creatures, I felt heartbroken that she was living alone. I did some research and found that when the Stone Zoo temporarily closed in 1990; it sent Kitubinissa to a zoo in Syracuse, NY. While there at some point, she became pregnant but died in childbirth.

Baby Kitubinissa filled me with joy when I was a child and my affection for her has stayed with me throughout my life. My time with her was only the first of many elephant encounters I've had. In my late 20s, as a river guide, I rafted on rivers through massive game preserves in Africa, where I observed herds of wild elephants roaming through the savannah, living the life that Kitubinissa should have had. How proudly they ruled over their homeland. Those full-grown healthy elephants were mighty enough to fend off all predators except one—human beings.

When I worked for the US government in Pakistan in the early 1980s, Pakistan's solitary elephant lived in miserable conditions in a zoo in their capital city. A few years later, I visited Sri Lanka for the annual Festival of the Tooth Relic, in which elephants covered with strings of colored light bulbs and bedecked with gaudy blankets and face coverings paraded through the streets of Kandy. The most majestic elephant earned the privilege of carrying a small box which displayed

Brenda Smith
Belfast, ME

a tiny fragment of the Lord Buddha's tooth. While there, I also visited a refuge for baby elephants orphaned by poachers who killed their mothers for their ivory tusks.

Sadly, I have reached the conclusion that human beings have not treated elephants kindly. Rampant poaching in both Africa and Asia has devastated the elephant populations on those continents. And the elephants who live in captivity in zoos around the world often bear physical and behavioral scars from isolation and confinement in tiny enclosures. My heart grieves that most of humankind does not appreciate nor care that the magnificent beauty and grace of the wild elephant's time on this planet is coming to an end. Personally, I can't bear the thought of a world in which the only elephants our children will know will be the fictional ones from storybooks.

***

Bunny L. Richards
Trescott Twp., ME

Moss

There is a piece of moss
unattached
among the long grass
in the field there.

I could smile today
but yesterday it rained
on the road,
in the woods
and on that piece of moss
breaking its marriage
with the rocks.

Sandy Conlon
Steamboat Springs, CO

Returning

On seeing Matt Smith's painting, ***Weathered****,*
which features a wooden structure from a long
ago time in a snowy field with distant mountains.
Matt is a nationally known professional artist.

In the first light hillsides teemed
with aspen trimmed in saffron and gold,
cottonwoods shimmered alizarin, crimson
and silver-streaked rocks and rills
like tungsten steel in the afternoon sun
reflected the passing day.

They might have said she's seen better days—
her timbers are all dried up,
seared in summer heat—so where's the life now,
the vibrant laughter, children at play?

Of course she ran the sheep and cows,
catered to the whinnying demands of horses,
invited neighbors for picnics, campfires,
Sunday dinners, sleigh rides, welcomed barn dances,
barbeques, birthdays, wedding feasts, and funerals.

She watched wind move down the mountain pass
across the quiet earth older than time itself.
It was a land of misery, a land of plenty
leveled by the winds and brought back
to what it once was.

Through the years, time and circumstance
lifted her from her moorings,
led her back to the beginning,
to the land she came to love.

Sandy Conlon
Steamboat Springs, CO

She saw the landscape lying fallow,
waiting for memory to be enlivened
by the nuance of perspective
and brushstrokes of immortality from the artist's hand.

***

Lou Bolster
Fairfield, IA

Fresh Snow

What is it about freshly fallen snow?

Maybe it's that I can see Angel foot prints easier.
And where the tips of their wings dust the earth.

Or, that the brilliant red of the cardinal
sitting in the barren viburnum bush
stands out more.

Or maybe it's the silence.
The silence that forces my ears
to calibrate anew and hear what I have forgotten.

Could it be that it's the brilliant white.
The unspoiled innocence.
Unadulterated by anything human.

Perhaps it is simpler.
Maybe I told myself I needed an excuse
to set aside my "to-do" list.
And breathe.
Settle down. Get comfortable.
And read.

Kitty Hartford
Boothbay Harbor, ME

When I'm Hurt

When I'm thirsty, I drink.
When I'm hungry, I eat.
When I'm tired, I sleep.
When I'm sad, I weep.

When I'm restless, I walk.
When I'm lonely, I talk.
When I'm joyful, I beam.
When I'm angry, I scream.

When I'm needy, I ask.
When I'm full, I give.
When I'm happy, I sing.
When I'm hurt, I...

When I'm hurt, I...
When I'm...
When I...
When...

***

Steve Troyanovich
Florence, NJ

whispers of sunset

like an eternity
of colors
gleaming your warmth
sunset falls dreaming
all over your touch

Helen Ackermann
Rothschild, WI

The Importance of the Written Word

During this past year, I have tried to rid the house of unnecessary items. I think it is called downsizing. We have in our possession many things that my father and mother saved. My father especially was a saver. Because of time, we did not downsize when we moved into our present home, twenty-five years ago. We just moved everything from our old home to the new one. At this time, it is not only downsizing but an "end of life" project. The story told by many elderly is that they don't want to burden their children with all that is in their house. Others simply say that their children will have to get a dumpster and deal with it. I am of the former group and am trying to lessen the burden.

Among the many items saved by my father are countless letters. Those of us who lived before the advent of modern technology found that letter writing was important. It was the way that people communicated. As I read over many of the letters I had an insight into my parents that I would never have known. My father saved all the letters written to him by my mother when they were dating. I found that she was a romantic and loving girlfriend. She had a sense of humor and displayed it in her letters to him. When I went away to college, I too received many letters. Since I am an only child, attending college was a big event for my parents. They missed me very much. Their way of keeping in touch was by the many letters they wrote. It was common for each of them to write and it was not unusual for a letter of ten to twelve pages to arrive. I am sure I read them at the time, but not the way I have been reading them now. If you can imagine, their letters were like a phone conversation. Although we had a phone in the old farm house and of course in the dorm where I lived, phone conversations were somewhat limited as many others wanted to use the phone as well. Letter writing seemed to be the choice of communication by my parents.

I feel very blest to have all of these letters. When we married and later had children, the letters continued. Reading them has given me a most profound understanding of the great love my parents had for me, my husband and our two sons. They shared who they were most intimately. The humor they shared came through in their letters. Their love for one another was a part of the letters. The frustrations they felt when dealing with relatives and others were also included in the letters. I don't think I would have understood my parents as much without these letters.

I have become a letter writer as well. Remembering people's birthday with a hand written card is part of who I am. Sending sympathy cards and notes is important to me. I have even committed myself to a letter a week to our grandson who is away in college. I have asked him to keep the letters as they will provide a source of family history for him when he is older. Keeping a journal for each of our grandsons is another way to keep family history alive.

It seems each of us is interested in finding our roots. Public television enables public figures to explore their past. Sites on the internet will help people trace their family tree. Many want to know how their past has influenced the person who they are now. I am certain that the reading of these many letters has given me a sense of who I am and my interest in writing. I was reassured through the written word how much I was loved. It also has enabled me to know my parents more intimately. I do hope that others find writing to be an important part of passing on family history. Although technology makes it easy to communicate, it does not necessarily convey what is expressed through the written word.

As I continue to sort through the many letters I have in my possession, my parents although dead for many years are more alive than ever. I am so very grateful.

Bill Herring
Minnetonka, MN

Shortly After He Died

Einstein's brain, about the size of a cantaloupe,
but infinitely more intelligent, was removed
from under the unruly white hair
that covered his scalp
like a forest fire gone out of control.
The melon, no longer thinking
about the fabric of time and space
or what keeps the obedient planets
on their leashes as they sniff
the paths around their stars,

or more immediately, what to have for lunch,
was photographed from various angles,
and I can imagine
one of them matted and framed and hanging
on a wall in the living room
of the Einstein home
next to the portraits of Hermann and Pauline
and other members of the family tree.

Once cooled to room temperature,
the brain was cut into cubes,
then placed in Mason jars,
the kind your great-grandmother kept,
covered in cobwebs on the shelves
in her pantry stocked with jams, marmalades
and other suspicious preserves.

A less than stellar finale to the man
who said, *The intuitive mind*
is a sacred gift. Who said, *Imagination*
is more important than knowledge.

Jayne Decker
Farmington, ME

For the Fisherman

A brief prose (perhaps a prayer)

November. Maine.
Rain saturates the earth.
A sound soothes from behind a window, tapping comfort
rhythm removed from any threat of elements.
The safety of glass.

Four men are missing.
My son, fishing from the same coast, is not waiting to hear
if they will be found.
Because he *knows* when a tattered lifeboat is recovered.
He *knows* with the assurance of one who has worn the
immersive suit
pulled frozen socks from his feet
broken ice out of his hair.

They are at the bottom of the ocean.

He tells me about the fishermen as I watch the rain,
holding a phone against my
face. They are lost or almost lost, like his friend pulled from
the sea, a man who
cut a rope to save his life as he tumbled overboard just a
few days earlier.
Now this other boat from the same harbor
a crew of four and a search that has lasted into the hours
of futile waiting.

Boats often have beautiful names
the names of women or the sentiment of journey.
Mates sometimes keep tokens in their pockets, perhaps a
coin or stone, a small

Jayne Decker
Farmington, ME

photo tucked in plastic buried deep in the folds of a shirt.
See that smile? The curl in her hair?
They are a rugged clan, softened only by what they carry, following the call to
haul traps or drag nets for days without land under their feet.
The choice in going to sea—money or generations of fishing, the love of a boat,
the salt smell that tastes like life—bands them together in knowing how to work
to the bone, sustain, survive until they can't.
Within a fierce monster of waves, an angry mouth of water in a storm that opens
its fury, the boat, no matter its size, is fragile.

A boat can be lost in minutes.

Some survive. Some return.

Rain. Or sun. Water in all its glory. A sky that melts a horizon. All you can see is
sea, a blue so cold and sharp, the color of broken glass.
At night, the crux of stars cradles the deck.
The same siren that calls them out has the power to swallow them whole.

The poetry of pain. Those of us left on land are the ones waiting. We only imagine
the moments of storm.
Widows have walked for centuries.
Fathers have prayed.
Mothers have accepted that those sons called to their boats
can't be held in the crutch of an arm.

We let them go, those of us waiting.

Jayne Decker
Farmington, ME

A man cuts a rope to save his life as he tumbles overboard.
        There is no choice in
who is taken. A man cuts a rope and survives.

***

Jean Biegun
Davis, CA

Spring Trail Reunion

Time now for Eden
to whoop up the earth,
rainbow banners to shoo
winter's black-white-gray.

Crown the royal trillium
glitter-gowned after rain,
and salute the young cattail parade
through the marsh.

Tip hat to dogwood buds
blushing debut joy,
and dance and stay dancing
until warblers wing you up
to be one of their own.

Sing May magnificent every day.
Rejoice that your spring
has come home.

Mikal Crawford
Damariscotta, ME

It's a secret!

"Tata," my three-year-old grandson asked his daddy, "what's a secret?" Tata is Croatian for daddy and Marko, my son-in-law, was born and raised in Croatia.

"It's something that you don't want everyone to know," Marko answered wondering where this was going.

"Okay."

"What's your secret, Luka?" Marko asked a few moments later.

Luka leaned over and whispered in his tata's ear, "I'm not going to take naps anymore."

Where did this come from? Luka occasionally brings home other words and phrases that make his parents chuckle. When he was two and a half, they asked if he wanted to wear his green jacket to daycare. He looked at them for a moment and replied, "Actually, not today."

This nap business could be a bit more challenging. I can just imagine my daughter Katie groaning when she got this news. Katie is the poster child for naps, always has been. Plus, she has a five-week-old newborn son who nurses every two hours, successfully invading her naptime for the foreseeable future.

As she was relaying this news about the secret to me, my first thought was, "Get a sailboat!" I drifted back in time to when she was about Luka's age. We lived by a lake in western Maryland then, and had a little Sunfish sailboat. I have loved to sail since forever (or at least ninth grade), and found it difficult to do at times with two little girls in the mix. Fortunately, I could take them over to my parents' house where our Sunfish waited on the beach. My older daughter would get interested in other things with her grandpa. Katie and I would escape on the water.

I put several square boat cushions in the little cockpit of

Mikal Crawford
Damariscotta, ME

the boat, snapped her green lifejacket securely in place and lifted her over the rail to settle in amid the padding. Raising the sail, I took hold of the tiller and shoved off from shore. Katie would be in that drowsy place after lunch, with a full tummy and heavy eyelids. As we glided away from the beach, she leaned against the cushions, brown eyes gently closing, sunhat shading her face, and we were off on another voyage. I tacked back and forth to get out of the cove, slow lazy turns, bouncing through waves from a few motor boats, and moving with the wind. Katie slept on. I loved being out there with her, sailing around for an hour or more with the water slipping beneath the hull as she slept peacefully. Such a pleasant memory of time spent on the water with my youngest child, sun warming my face as the breeze tossed my hair. We had a number of such sails over the course of the summer. To be honest, though, she was an easy napper who rarely put up much fuss, and never on the sailboat.

Snap back from memory lane to today, and her son, Luka, who announced he wasn't going to take naps anymore. What are parents to do with that one? They don't live near a lake, and don't own a sailboat. Katie tells me she and Marko read somewhere that children tend to stop napping around age three. (Get a sailboat, I think again.)

"I wonder if he'll nap at daycare," I muse.

"I guess we'll find out on Monday," she says.

Sitting here writing this, I wonder if the aversion to naps at home is, in part, a response to not wanting to miss out on something, or have his baby brother do something that he doesn't get to do. He's had a few meltdowns since Nikola was born, all to be expected. It's hard sharing space and parents with a newcomer. He's also three-years-old and asserting his independence. There are alternatives to a nap, like quiet play in one's room. Or snuggling with Mommy while she naps, though I'm not sure how that would go.

I think having a baby during the covid debacle is an act of raw courage. And this little family of four has successfully

Mikal Crawford
Damariscotta, ME

navigated a bout with covid that Luka brought home from daycare. It's a strange time for everyone and I give them high marks for hanging in there and sailing through some pretty rough waters. I have full confidence that they will figure this out too.

The latest update is that Luka is napping at daycare, BARELY. Who can predict where this nap business will go? Maybe only Luka knows for sure. He's not telling though. Shhhh...it's a secret!

***

Roselyn Stewart
Brookfield WI

Rain

I take a ride in
the rain.
A pensive, melancholy
takes hold as rusty
brown leaves scatter in
the wind.
Up ahead my mailbox
stands like a soldier in the
rain.
I pull up close, lower the
hatch and retrieve my mail.
On my way back to the garage
rain dances in puddles.
I watch from inside as
leaves drop from the trees,
auburn, red, gold, and warm
and dry within, I witness the
day unfold.

San D. Hasselman
Boothbay Harbor, ME

Me and Mary Ann

She is tucked in, neat as a pin.
I'm not
She is wedded to her past, connected to her chums.
I'm not
She is detailed, practical and deliberate.
I'm not

I'm short, round and boisterous.
She's not
I'm adrift with no linear past.
She's not
I'm artsy, unpredictable and messy.
She's not

Together we author a novel friendship.
We are
United in our common disquiet cocoons,
We are
List makers, organizers and motivators,
We are
Both seeking serenity.

Susan Blackwell
Albuquerque, NM

A Visit from Santa and His Reindeer

Christmas in New England has always been one of my fondest childhood memories. It's no surprise that this time of year evokes such warm and cozy feelings as I recall the pristine beauty of snow-covered trees and the creamy lusciousness of hot chocolate, adorned with a generous serving of whipped cream. I also loved the evergreen fragrance of our Christmas tree and our special holiday treats, including my nana's heavenly butterball cookies and my mom's magnificent eggnogs that she magically turned into enchanting delights with food coloring.

At the age of eight, I was excited that Santa Claus would soon be arriving in his giant sleigh with all the toys I wanted —especially the Tiny Tears doll that actually cried real tears after giving her a bottle. Only this year, things were a little different due to the rumors I heard about Santa not being real from some kids with older siblings.

I still wanted to believe in Santa but I worried the rumors were true. Thankfully, I didn't have much time to dwell on the existence of Santa because I was busy throughout December with my third-grade school work, rehearsing for our school's Christmas show, making wreaths with my Girl Scout troop, and making and buying Christmas gifts.

The 1961 holiday season is particularly memorable because I experienced two Christmas miracles that year. The first one occurred while shopping for family gifts. As I walked up and down the aisles of Woolworth's in downtown Framingham, I began loading items into my hand-held basket, hoping the dollar I had in my pocket would cover the cost of everything.

After choosing a gift for each family member, I began to calculate the total cost before approaching the cashier. When I saw that I didn't have enough money, I sadly realized I

Susan Blackwell
Albuquerque, NM

needed to return some gifts and look for less expensive options. As I began walking toward the back of Woolworth's, I silently said a prayer, asking for help with the situation. When I arrived at the back of the store I looked down, and to my amazement, I spotted a dollar bill lying on the floor. I was shocked, and considered it a true miracle since I had just prayed for additional cash to purchase the gifts I had so carefully chosen.

As the December days flew by, I began to feel more concerned about whether Santa was real. I didn't say anything to anyone because I thought saying it out loud might ruin Christmas.

On Christmas Eve at bedtime, I tried to imagine Santa riding through the dark night sky with Rudolph leading the way. My sister, Sandi, and I put out cookies and milk for Santa by the fireplace in our living room and left a bucket of water and carrots by the front door for the reindeer. I could only hope that our efforts weren't in vain.

As it turned out, Santa had his work cut out for him that Christmas Eve due to a blizzard that dumped two feet of snow in our area. I'm sure he was glad to have Rudolph guiding his sleigh through the stormy night.

The next morning Sandi and I were up bright and early to see what Santa had left. I was thrilled to find the Tiny Tears doll I wanted. Our Christmas stockings were filled with all kinds of goodies, including Spoolies to curl my hair, a Life Savers Christmas book filled with rolls of assorted Life Savers, bubble gum, and Play-Doh.

Sandi and I were also excited to find that Santa had brought us skis. The timing was perfect with all the snow that now graced our yard. We certainly got our wish for a white Christmas!

With the excitement of opening our gifts, I wasn't thinking about Santa's existence that morning. When Sandi and I noticed the empty glass of milk and plate, I silently thought that either of my parents could have eaten the cookies and

Susan Blackwell
Albuquerque, NM

enjoyed the glass of milk we left for Santa.

The real surprise occurred when I walked over to the front door and noticed spilled water, hay, and dirt on the carpet. I couldn't believe my eyes! Given the mess I was seeing, it could only have been made by the reindeer because my mom was such a meticulous housekeeper. There was no way my parents would deliberately throw dirt and hay on the floor. As I stared at the smudged dirt and spilled water on the carpet that morning, I realized this was my second Christmas miracle—one that confirmed the true existence of Santa and his reindeer.

***

Thomas Peter Bennett
Silver Spring, MD

Audubon in Florida

(April 1832)

Here I am in the Floridas . . .
which from my childhood
I have consecrated in my imagination
as the Garden of the United States . . .
Mr. Bartram was the first
to call this a garden,
But he is to be forgiven:
he was an enthusiastic botanist,
and rare plants,
in the eyes of such a man.
Convert a wilderness
At once into a garden.

John T. Hagan
Springboro, OH

You Were Just a Yellow Cat

You were just a yellow cat, bought for a buck at the animal
shelter.
You were just a yellow cat who made us roar in laughter
with your kitten antics.
You were just a yellow cat who, well fed with Little Friskies,
still begged at the kitchen door.
You were just a yellow cat whose plaintive squeals made
her vet-check drive a virtual odyssey.
You were just a yellow cat who warmed herself on the
horses' backs in winter.
You were just a yellow cat who walked the paddock fence
and licked our faces with your sandpaper tongue.
You were just a yellow cat who charmed children and
grandchildren and rode on their shoulders.
You were just a yellow cat who instinctively knew animal-
loving neighbors and visitors.
You were just a yellow cat who played tag with the Border
Collie and dodged her under the John Deere mower.
You were just a yellow cat whose hayloft bed gave her a
"cat's-eye" view of the dooryard activity.
You were just a yellow cat who curled on laps and gave us
those soothing moments of serenity.
You were just a yellow cat whose passing causes an ache in
our hearts and yields a torturous longing.
You were just a yellow cat. No, you were our Frannie!

John Gillespie
Camden, ME

she carried her death like a mule

she carried her death like a mule
standing before us with her children

a holocaust survivor without the tattoo,
a clothed skeleton on the path to the beach.

we stood, somehow embarrassed,
words clawing their way out of our papier-mache mouths
and dropping into the sand at our feet

and death, with the slightest shrug of his shoulder,
dragging her from us toward an impossible goodbye.

***

Abby Staberg
Brunswick, ME

August at the Farm

In a spectacle of wonder
shadows whistle through the thunder
as we laze away from under
getting honeysuckle high.

Heavy heat and scattered showers
—sudden storms that rage for hours—
nurture fields of grains and flowers
clover   lily   daisy   rye.

the late Corinne Eastman Davis
Montpelier, VT

Love Song

If all the dawns of earth
Are blotted out,
and every hope and prayer
Becomes a doubt;

If land is swallowed by
A tideless sea,
And night follows night
Endlessly;

If planets thunder down
In mighty quake,
And the skeleton of earth
Begins to break;

My love for you, lingering
On in space,
Will listen for your voice,
Will seek your face.

***

Steve Troyanovich
Florence, NJ

in thulean stillness...

wounded butterflies
hug shapes
of melancholy fanes
beyond lethean dawns
fading into slumber
where time dreams...

Alvaro de Araujo
Garland, TX

Inheritance

Fallsville lay in a quiet corner of Northwest Texas, at least twenty-five miles from the nearest city in any direction. It couldn't be found on any road map. Main Street was the town's only paved road, lined on one side by timeworn buildings—a bakery, a supermarket, five small shops and a bicycle dealer—and on the other side by a gas station, a tire repair shop and a pharmacy. The last fast-food restaurant had ceased operations long ago, leaving Bob's Hot Pot as the only coffee shop in town. The antiquated, privately owned gas station ran out of fuel at least once every two months. The post office was a one-man operation where residents could pick up their mail at its small crowded room once a week.

***

Black numbers and letters on a white rectangular sign by the side of the road, at the entrance to the town, indicated the population count. It was updated once a year by its oldest resident, ninety-two-year-old former mayor Bret Simpson. The new count stood at 776, lower than the previous year's numbers; fewer births and a higher mortality rate were responsible for the first sharp decrease in its history. There were also two still unexplained disappearances, and the relocation of a family of three who had moved south earlier that summer. It had been quite an exciting year for this small town where the unusual seldom happened.

The changing of the tally was an important event for the town's people; a ceremony, in fact, that attracted a large number of residents. Birth certificates for the newborn and death certificates for the departed were required for the official count, as well as farewell letters from those moving away. They cheered for the newborn and prayed for the deceased in what was an old, solemn tradition.

The two missing men represented a problem for the local authorities: Should they or should they not be subtracted from the population records?

“Yes,” weighed in Max Trevor, the chief of police, at a town meeting. “They aren’t here, are they? If they ever reappear, and I hope they will—we’ll add them back into the count.”

“Absolutely not,” contested the town’s only lawyer. “Legally, they’re still alive.”

The discussion went on for some time, with the lawyer losing the argument at the end.

***

Max Trevor had been Fallsville’s chief of police for the last fifteen years. Although only forty-eight, he looked much older due to his wrinkled face and a full head of grey hair. Indeed, in his younger years at the Austin Police Academy they had nicknamed him “Old Bones.”

During that year’s ceremony Max noticed Billy Boulder involved in an animated conversation with Helga, the wife of Herman Schmidt, one of the men who had vanished several months back. That dialogue struck him as odd because Helga and Billy had never been friends. In fact, Max believed they barely knew each other.

Thirty-eight-year-old Billy was a high school drop-out who did not hold a job. He subsisted supported by a small fortune bequeathed to him in a trust fund. Some twenty years earlier he had inherited from his parents the century-old mansion atop the hill where he now lived alone. He was single, a quiet man of few words who had no friends. Most everybody in town knew who he was but Billy didn’t know them except to say “hello” when their paths crossed on the way to the fruit-and-vegetable market or the grocery store. Six-foot-four, 300-pound Billy never smiled. People felt uneasy in his presence. Some of them, including Max, suspected Billy as having had something to do with the death of his parents. Those murders remained unsolved.

Getting closer to Billy and Helga, the chief of police was surprised when he heard them talking in a foreign language. Helga and her missing husband were German immigrants, so Max could understand that. But Billy Boulder? Billy could hardly speak English correctly . . .!

Max approached them, extending a hand to the woman. "Hello, Helga, I haven't seen you for some time. How've you been?" he asked ever so politely.

"All right, I guess. Have you any news about my Herman?"

"No, I'm sad to say. But we're still working on the case full time."

Helga nodded quietly. "I know you are."

Max looked at Billy then back at Helga. "I'm sorry to intrude like this."

"Not at all," she replied. "We're just chatting. This young man wanted to practice his newly learned language."

"Hello, Billy." Max did not offer his hand.

"Hello, Chief."

"You surprise me. Where did you learn German?"

"Reading books at home. Anything wrong with that?"

"No, not really. I was just curious."

Billy dropped his cigarette butt on the ground and stepped on it. "Have you found out anything about Neil Robertson's disappearance?"

"Not a clue," Max replied.

"Too bad. He was a great chess player."

"Yes, I know. We've played many times in the past. Only once I managed to give him a checkmate, but only because he was drunk at the time . . ." he chuckled. "I really enjoyed those matches."

"Well, he's not irreplaceable, you know?"

"How do you mean?"

"I can play just as good as he did."

"*You*? I didn't know you played chess."

"Not until recently," Billy said with a little quirk to one side of his mouth.

"How did you . . ." he paused. "Wait, don't tell me. You learned at home, reading books."

"You're right." He crossed his arms. "Why don't you come over some day?" He grew more arrogant. "I can beat you."

Max had wanted to go back to the mansion for some time now, and that was a great opportunity. "I might just do that," he said. "How about this Saturday?"

"I'll be home. Come in the afternoon." Billy turned to Helga. "Thank you for the chat, Mrs. Schmidt. I have to go now. *Auf wiedersehen.*" And he was gone.

"I'm glad you came by, Max," Helga said, wringing her hands, once Billy was out of earshot. "That man gives me the creeps."

"Why's that?"

"The words he used . . . the perfection of his German . . . I don't know. He scares me, Max. He sounded just like my Herman!"

They talked for a while longer and at the end of the ceremony people started going back to their homes. Not Max Trevor. He drove back to his office to review Herman Schmidt's case, together with that of Neil Robertson's, the plumber who had also vanished. The chief of police had a gut feeling the two cases were related, although he had no evidence to corroborate that. He needed to find a common denominator. In Max Trevor's mind, if there was validity in gut feelings, Billy Boulder was that link. But how was he involved? Billy had said that Herman *was* a good player, as if knowing he'd never be found, he recalled.

Early on in the investigation he had talked with Billy's part-time maid. She told him then that Herman had been at the mansion talking business the day before going missing. Could Neil have been at the house before his disappearance,

Alvaro de Araujo
Garland, TX

too?

***

Saturday afternoon the chief of police drove to the mansion. Billy Boulder wasn't home.

"Well, I was invited," he explained to the maid who answered the door. "I think I'll just wait for him," he continued as he walked past her and into the house.

She closed the door behind him. "I don't know how long he's gonna be."

"Well, it doesn't matter. Where did he go?"

"Beats me. He never tells me anything," she said, shrugging her shoulders. "It's only 'Good morning,' when I come in, 'Don't touch the freezer,' whenever he goes out somewhere, and 'Good night,' when I go home. That's the whole damn conversation."

"What's in the freezer?"

"Meat, I reckon." The woman brought him a cup of coffee. "Or at least it used to be six or seven months ago." She resumed her work dusting the furniture. "He's been acting kind of funny since then."

"How so?" They walked into the kitchen, and Max put down his hardly touched cup of coffee on the marble countertop.

"I used to do all the cooking myself before, you see, but now he won't let me touch the meat. He prepares and cooks it himself, and then eats the whole thing." She shook her head. "I'm not allowed to have any part of it. Ain't that weird?"

"It is strange," Max agreed, and then changed the subject. "I'm sure you've heard about Neil."

"The plumber? Yeah, I heard he skipped town. Did you catch him?"

"He didn't skip town; he had no reason for that. He's just missing. But tell me something. Was he here about three

Alvaro de Araujo
Garland, TX

months ago?"

"Lemme think." She stopped her work and rubbed the back of her neck. "I reckon so. We had a leak in the basement at one time. A busted pipe or sumpin'. . .yes, he was here then. I can't tell you the exact date but it was 'bout that time."

Max opened the freezer. All seven shelves were stuffed with brown paper wrapped packages. "There is enough food here for an army," he commented. "What are these packages?"

"That's the darn meat I told ya."

Max thought about opening one of them but changed his mind when he heard Billy coming through the front door. He closed the freezer and walked out of the kitchen. The two men met in the living room and exchanged a few words before Billy suggested they sit at the dining room table.

After a while the maid followed them there. "I'm done, Mr. Boulder. See you Monday."

"Good night," Billy replied without looking at her.

She looked at Max, her eyes saying, "What did I tell you?"

She picked up her weekly pay, which was always left on the coffee table in the living room, counted it, and then left.

A few minutes later Billy brought the chessboard to the table and they set the pieces. Max drew the blacks, so Billy was first to play. He advanced the bishop's pawn two squares.

The English Opening, Neil's favorite first move! The sudden thought exploded in Max's mind like a flare, and then it dawned on him—the common denominator he was after: Billy seemed to have "inherited" the knowledge of the missing men somehow; first, by mastering Herman's proficiency in the German language, and now by acquiring Neil's chess expertise. How had he accomplished that in such a short time? Not by reading books, that's for sure.

The freezer! Max's heartbeat skyrocketed. *Was it possible*?

Alvaro de Araujo
Garland, TX

They made a few moves. The match proceeded slowly as Max's mind was no longer in the game. His opponent observed him with cold eyes.

"It's your move, Chief," he said in an even colder voice.

After making his move and pushing back his chair, Max told Billy to go ahead and figure out his next play, explaining he was thirsty, and then adding: "Don't bother getting up, Billy. I'll get some water myself."

He started to the kitchen before Billy could say anything. Opening the freezer as quietly as he could, he chose a package and unwrapped it. It was just an ordinary piece of meat; it could be anything. He opened another package, and what he saw made him gag.

A slight noise from behind put Max on alert and made him whirl around, his right hand reaching for his service revolver.

***

Months later a group of people stood in front of the police station, listening to what the former mayor had to say:

". . . and now, folks of Fallsville, here is the big news. It's been some time since the disappearance of our Max Trevor. Of course, we all miss him and hope that he'll show up again soon, alive and well. However, life must go on. Therefore, as of today, I'm happy to present a man who has surprised me with a profound knowledge of criminology and a solid understanding of the law. He swears he'll do everything in his power to solve the mystery of these disappearances and make sure that it doesn't happen again here in our beloved town. And I believe him."

The former mayor raised his hands, waiting until all the talking and humming subsided, before introducing the new entrant:

"Ladies and gentlemen, meet our new chief of police, Billy Boulder!"

Deborah Loomis Lafond
Raymond, ME

Lake Love

Liquid confetti from a gentle spring rain
dappled the lake.
Two loons danced a courtship samba
chuffing and cooing.
He, preening and performing.
She, demurely pretending not to notice,
Then sidling up to him
as if to say,
"I am impressed, but not today."
The rain became a shower and then, a torrent.
The loon pair swam away
together moving to the rhythm of nature.

***

Steve Troyanovich
Florence, NJ

variation on a translation

for Rodolfo Alonso

yesterday's escape
into cantos
of lost tomorrows...
the first songs
of oblivion
feel eternity
in your voice

Grace B. Sheridan
Cutler, ME

Of a Well

Michael and Candice are home
overlooking the bay again:

Home to their salted cape with its ell
connected to the barn on the ridge,

Home to the clothes-pinned line out back
suspended between two cross-armed posts,

Home to the wheelbarrow and rusty hoe
leaning against a compost pile.

A profusion of window-box petunias
match red and white Adirondack chairs

but Michael and Candice choose
the side by side cushioned rockers

just inside the open barn door
far from schoolhouse mathematics.

Tonight the sunset is lavender.
Perhaps it will rain tomorrow.

That will help the well
as coming home always does.

They will be back in September
to bag up the potatoes

and again in October
to take up dahlia bulbs.

Kate Kearns
Scarborough, ME

Trees Know When the Days Grow Shorter

My girl reaches for my hand,
        along our boot-trod trail. My eye

scouts the crows, which don't
        fly from us but look down large beaks

and resume their black passage
        through conifer tops. Do they hear

the sap slowing for winter? *Ma*!
        Ma! the crows take up a racket,

a warning of our presence, though
        they're used to us by now. No,

it's her voice seeking me by that
        other name. My ear requires the birds,

can't help it. They'll take needles
        the pines don't keep and stay

in these woods 'til spring in secret haunts.
        This morning she twirled our driveway,

down and back, down and back, down,
        sock-footed and swift as a maple seed

descending. I started to tell her
        to put on shoes. I stopped myself.

For the first time, on this walk—I'm not sorry—
        I want her to prefer the crows.

Kristina Branch
Boothbay Harbor, ME

That Shade of Red

She didn't mean to snoop. She wasn't that sort of wife. But she just happened to come across the handkerchief when she was organizing his desk drawers as she often did when he went out. She noticed that he rarely thanked her, just one more thing she wasn't pleased about.

When she first met Jim, she liked that he danced well and laughed a lot. But now he seemed preoccupied, remote. He put her off when she asked him where he'd gone and what *he'd done.* Same old, same old, he would say.

And what bothered her the most was that he forgot to do what mattered to her. Like looking at their albums. Like doing chores on weekends. She had to mention things a thousand times. And on their wedding anniversary—nothing.

She found the handkerchief inside the cover of his checkbook. Unfolding it, she spread it out across his blotter. Then she gasped. Below his monogram was a bright red trace of lipstick. Her hands went cold. The scarlet shade was garish, not like the pastel colors she preferred.

How dare he cheat? How could he? She wouldn't stand for it! Tears flooded her face.

When Jim came in from his walk, he found her standing near the door. Wordlessly, she flung the handkerchief on the floor before him.

"Cleaning up my desk again?" he asked. He picked up the handkerchief and tucked it carefully in his breast pocket.

"Throw away that thing!" she cried. "Get rid of it right now!"

"I'm sorry, dear," he replied. "I can't. It reminds me of you, years ago."

"No, no! Don't lie to me!" she cried. "That lipstick's hideous! I don't wear that shade of red!"

"But you used to," he answered. "You loved that color.

Kristina Branch
Boothbay Harbor, ME

Don't you remember?"

And when she numbly shook her head, he reached out and held her quivering hands, warming them between his palms.

"Please, my dear," he begged, "don't you remember our first night? Please, dear, don't you?"

***

Sylvia Little-Sweat
Wingate, NC

Pilgrimage to Rome

Consumptive death, a conflagration of wasted breath,
a living death in a house above the Spanish Steps
where Keats keeps vigil. A sudden wind can send
the fountain's splash from the piazza to an open
window above where Severn watches night after
night by candlelight as Keats fingers the cool
cornelian stone from Fanny Brawne like a rosary.

Did the nightingale
sing your spirit home at dark
as you once had hoped?

Walled in by stone, the cemetery lies on a verdant hill
where fields of flowers bloom in the Roman spring and
feral cats roam at will around the Pyramid of Cestius.
Still, unexpected snow can entomb a tomb, induce
a cosmic sleep and hush the clamor of unrequited love.
In the vaulted silence of the tomb Fanny's letters—
sealed still—lie mute, consigned like love itself to time.

Lou Bolster
Fairfield, IA

Miracles

I witnessed a Miracle today.
Well, I think I did.

To be clear, a Miracle is
"a surprising and welcome event
that is not explicable by natural or scientific
laws and is therefore considered
to be the work of a divine agency."

So says the *Oxford Language Dictionary*.

For me, not being an expert in the laws
of Science or Nature, I cannot explain
really any of what I witness.
So. Miracles.

Things I too easily take for granted.
The Blue of the Sky.
The wind.
That my feet go where I want them to.
So many others.
Or when I Feel and sometimes
tears come to help move a feeling along.

Oh yes.
Miracles.

Robert B. Moreland
Pleasant Prairie, WI

Premonitions

I
Bison, his head bowed somehow perceiving,
brown eyes deep, blinks twice. Cold mist thick,
droplets pause grapelike on long russet hairs
until his horned head shakes, dismissing them.

Somehow, he knows. Eighteen forty-two blizzard
on the Platte River when prairie grasses sweet
fed all the countless minions till late fall's kiss.
Is it instinct? Bows his head, recalls freedom.

II
Burr oak amidst cornfield stubble reaches;
branches fractal, shadow against the mist.
Busy road, morning rush, no one sees him.
A hundred winters now and he knows, too.

III
Misting drizzle coats the commuting cars,
headlights dance while Bach cantata soothes him.
Too many deadlines and commitments, he
rehearses his nine 'o clock crisis speech.

Weatherman, much like the state senator,
pontificates so certain, all the while
clueless, bound in his meaningless data
huge blizzard looming that he cannot see.

Katharina Keoughan
Newcastle, ME

Merry Christmas

It was cold out. Annie buttoned her coat, grabbed her apartment key and the stack of envelopes sitting on the side table. As Annie stepped into the hall, she could feel Mrs. Murray's inquisitive eyes on the addressed, stamped wad of cards she was holding. "Good morning, Annie, looks like you have lots of friends to send Christmas cards to," her neighbor chirped.

Annie had patience, and patience is what was necessary in dealing with Mrs. Murray, who had nothing else to do all day but greet whomever she could catch in the hall. "Well, actually I don't know any of these people," Annie said with a smirk.

Mrs. Murray laughed and said, "You are so silly." Annie returned her laugh and headed out to the street.

Annie really did not know the people she was mailing the twenty-five cards to. She had no connection to them, and she certainly did not put her return address on the envelope. Yes, the city name was on the postmark; however, with two million in the borough, the cards certainly could not be traced. Annie considered it a hobby, sending Christmas cards to perfect strangers. Only in her imagination could she see them opening the card, seeing the signature, "With best wishes, Annie," and wondering who they knew named Annie. She delighted in the thought that they would ponder her name for days, maybe weeks. They would examine the envelope for clues, check their address books, ask their relatives, and lie awake trying to remember associates, or clerks, or clients, or just anybody they had ever had any contact with by the name of Annie. This simple thing gave Annie enormous pleasure.

You may wonder how Annie found the lucky recipients. She thought of them as lucky recipients. The recipients

Katharina Keoughan
Newcastle, ME

might have considered themselves tortured victims. The process of gathering names and addresses was an important part of the pleasure for Annie. In the evenings, alone, after a day of working as a librarian, Annie would scour small-town newspapers all over the country. Local stories highlighted citizens whose address could be found with other internet searches. They did not know anything about Annie, but she knew they had helped at the church supper, worked as a volunteer firefighter, or led the Boy Scouts in the local parade.

The post box was only a block away. Annie held the cards to her chest, with anticipation of their arrival. She dropped the envelopes one by one into the slot. As Annie witnessed the last envelope disappear, she considered the possibility of Easter cards.

***

Allison Childs Wells
Gardiner, ME

Chickadees

Stones in the garden. Flowering
clusters of ginseng. The sea's
bubbling edge, tide bright
shells, opals, quartz. Silk
tufts of milkweed, distant
clouds. Leaves on a fluttering aspen
only the ready can see.

Cordula Mathias
Trevett, ME

The Sister's Name

We know about Abel and Cain
But what was the sister's name?

On the stone steps
Looming above me
He held a ski boot
In his hand

I remember the fear
But never knew
What his rage
Was about

I remember the
Pain
When the fierce blow
Came

Not my first beating

The child had
Murder in his heart

A vicious boy—
My brother
Who wanted to rid
Himself of a sister

Allison Childs Wells
Gardiner, ME

Silver

Some nights are
silver, lacing a way
through long, exhaled breath.
That catch beyond the hand
like sand sifts to a depth
we sleep for.

The song of silver is sun-warmed
tinkling over rocks,
the peel and sweep
of missing things.

Some bow to it, knees and palms
boring into stacks of vague wishes.
They slurp from pools of names
they think spell silver.

Others lie on their backs,
waiting, waiting for silver
to dizzy their spin. The stars are
too far, they know it. Their hearts
are dry.

Somewhere an abyss fills
with consequence, wisdom, folly.
It swallows all three as they swim
toward dream's silvery shore.

Juliana L'Heureux
Topsham, ME

Driving on Henrietta Lacks Way

I drive the Henrietta Lacks Way when traveling from Maryland's upper eastern shore, where my son lives, to visit my family and friends in Dundalk, an urban town located in Baltimore County, adjacent to the city. This piece of the Broening Highway leads me, literally, to where I grew up in Logan Village. Henrietta Lacks Way is a piece of road that extends from the exit ramp off of the Francis Scott Key Bridge, heading out of Sparrows Point, where the Bethlehem Steel Mills were once located. Ultimately, the entire length of road ends on Dundalk Avenue.

Henrietta Lacks Way was renamed at the place where the road passes an African American segregated middle class neighborhood called Turner Station.

Henrietta Lacks is the woman who is known in biological laboratories throughout the world as "HeLa." She was actually a young African American mother whose biography and extraordinary medical history are described in the bestselling biographical book by Rebecca Skloot and the movie produced by Oprah Winfrey, both of them titled *The Immortal Life of Henrietta Lacks.*

Johns Hopkins Hospital in Baltimore wrote about Henrietta Lacks on the hospital's website. In *Honoring the Legacy of Henrietta Lacks,* Johns Hopkins Hospital describes a young African American mother of five who visited the hospital in 1951, to see the renowned gynecologist named Dr. Howard Jones. At the time, the Johns Hopkins Hospital was one of only a very few hospitals in Baltimore to treat poor African Americans. Sadly, a large, malignant tumor was identified on her cervix.

As medical records show, Mrs. Lacks underwent radium treatments for her cancer. This was the best medical treatment available at the time for this terrible disease.

Juliana L'Heureux
Topsham, ME

What is extraordinary about this rare medical history is what happened to the cancer cells that were saved from the tumor. A sample of the cells retrieved during a biopsy were given to Dr. George Gey, who was a prominent cancer and virus researcher at Johns Hopkins. Dr. Gey was collecting cells from all patients, regardless of their race or socioeconomic status. He came to work and study at Johns Hopkins Hospital because, he believed, he could help to find a cure for this disease, if he could grow the cancer cells in a test tube.

Nevertheless, each sample he received quickly died. Except for the cells he received from Mrs. Lacks. They were unlike any of the others he had ever seen. Her cells did not die. Instead, Mrs. Lack's cells doubled every 20 to 24 hours.

Today, these incredible cells are "HeLa" cells, using the first two letters of Henrietta's first and last names. They are used in laboratories to study the effects of toxins, drugs, hormones and viruses on the growth of cancer cells without experimenting on humans. They have been used to test the effects of radiation and poisons, to study human genetics, to learn more about how viruses work, and they were crucial in the development of the polio and COVID-19 vaccines. But, Johns Hopkins did not reveal the identity of Henrietta Lacks. She and her family did not know about how her cells were the subject of research.

I never knew Mrs. Lacks, because when I worked at Johns Hopkins Hospital in the middle 1960s, she had already died on October 4, 1951, at the age of 31, long before I was employed there. But, her cells continue to impact the world to this day. In fact, hers were the first cells that could be easily shared and multiplied in a lab setting. "Johns Hopkins never sold or profited from the discovery or distribution of HeLa cells," claims the website. "Johns Hopkins does not own the rights to the HeLa cell line. Rather, Johns Hopkins offered HeLa cells freely and widely for scientific research."

Johns Hopkins admits that Henrietta Lacks' family mem-

Juliana L'Heureux
Topsham, ME

bers should have been informed about the research and what the cells were used for, out of respect for them, their privacy and their personal interests. Using Henrietta Lacks' cells in research was an acceptable and legal practice in the 1950s, but such a practice would not happen in American hospitals today, without the patient's consent.

Henrietta Lacks, her extraordinary history and the amazing HeLa cells are now classic subjects studied in medical ethics classes.

I am stunned by this amazing story. One unlikely heroine from Turner Station has positively impacted untold thousands of biological research projects and supported many life-saving medical technologies.

Henrietta Lacks, via her extraordinary living cells, has an "immortal life." Her story is as startling as finding one rare pearl in a stack of shucked oysters.

Yet, every time I inevitably pass Turner Station on Henrietta Lacks Way, I think about the other young women who I met while working at Johns Hopkins Hospital on a generously funded federal public health research grant. The thousands of clients in the research grant I worked on were all African Americans, men and women, who were subject to experimentation, just because of their race. None of the research conducted on this grant was invasive, but the fact is, the subjects did not know about how the blood samples they gave were being used.

Turner Station, where Henrietta Lacks and her family lived, was more or less in the backyard of Logan Village. Although I frequently drove by this neighborhood while growing up, we very seldom interacted because the 1950's and 60's had created two distinct communities, even though we shared the same 21222 zip code. There are still rows of chain link fences around the perimeter of Turner Station. Yes, it is an African American ghetto, but it has always been a fairly quiet residential neighborhood, with clean houses and narrow streets. You really have to know the neighborhood is there, because it is protected from view by a huge masonry wall constructed along a large part of the outer perimeter. The wall is a formidable barrier, separating the clustered small houses from the road. Inside the ghetto are churches, sidewalks, a library and even a small beach park located along Bear Creek and the Patapsco Rivers.

After Henrietta Lacks died in 1951, her family continued to live in Turner Station without any knowledge about how their mother's cells survived. In fact, the family was unaware about this astonishing history until a writer named Michael Rogers, from *Rolling Stone* magazine showed up there one day to write an investigative report about the origin of the HeLa cells. He published the article in 1976, titled "Finding Henrietta Lacks." Skloot later picked up this investigative story from where Rogers left off, because she wanted to know what happened to the Lacks family. She visited people in Turner Station who knew the family and followed every lead until, eventually, Henrietta's daughter, named Deborah, began to talk to her.

Incredibly, the Henrietta Lacks cells are still growing in medical research labs around the world. Some were even sent into space, to see if they grew in a zero gravity environment.

In my mind, Henrietta Lacks is more than one young African American woman and mother. Rather, she is among hundreds of others who were also the subjects of medical research at Johns Hopkins Hospital. In fact, while reading Rebecca Skloot's riveting medical biography about Henrietta and the HeLa cells, I experienced some professional flashbacks, because the non-fiction ethics thriller actually happened to occur in my home town of Dundalk, where Turner Station is located.

What happened to Henrietta Lacks is as compelling a story about medical ethics as the history of the Tuskegee experiment was, with unauthorized research on the community of men who were deceived into believing that they were

Juliana L'Heureux
Topsham, ME

being cured of syphilis. The Tuskegee Study of Untreated Syphilis was research conducted between 1932 and 1972, by the United States Public Health Service and the Centers for Disease Control and Prevention, on a group of nearly 400 African American men with syphilis. The intent of the study was to record the natural history of syphilis in African Americans.

Henrietta Lacks' cervical cancer was one woman's unique circumstance, but her story represents decades of untold other situations where the poor and medically underserved populations were often cared for by medical students and public health researchers. Their stories will never be told. An understanding about how African Americans were often used in medical research without knowing about it, gives us a better understanding about why many in this group are cynical about accepting vaccines today.

Yet, Henrietta Lacks has justifiably risen to the status of a medical heroine. In death, her cells have lived and helped medical scientists throughout the world. HeLa cells were important in the research to eradicate polio in most of the world, because they rapidly multiplied and thereby proved to be ideal for the vaccine testing.

Although Johns Hopkins claims that no money was made by using HeLa cells, the fact is, many public health research grants received untold amounts of money, as a result of having those cells. Undoubtedly, the research generated by the HeLa cells made money through indirect access obtained from third party contracts.

But, the Lacks family never received compensation for Henrietta's cells, even though the research with them continues to this day.

Today human experiments cannot be conducted without documented and complete transparency about the risks and benefits being disclosed to the research participants.

In the conclusion of the Henrietta Lacks' biography, Skloot summarizes how the Lacks family members felt about

Juliana L'Heureux
Topsham, ME

their mother's legacy. Henrietta's cells, which contain the DNA of her family members, are still living. Even knowing what they finally learned about their mother, the Lacks family does not want to cause problems for science, said her son, named Sonny. "I'm proud of my mother and what she's done for science. I just hope Hopkins and some of the other folks who benefited off her cells will do something to honor her and make right with the family."

When I drive the Henrietta Lacks Way, my thoughts extend to expressions of appreciation. I want to thank the young mother from Turner Station who contributed so much to advance the study of cell research. I always say, "Thank you, Henrietta Lacks," when I drive by Turner Station. In so doing, I recall the faces of other young African American women and men who I can recall receiving treatments at Johns Hopkins Hospital, who were very likely enrolled in research projects. We will never know who they were.

***

Sally Belenardo
Branford, CT

No Spring

The older I get,
when winter ends I've less and
less Spring in my step.

Judith L. Braun
Alfred, ME

Quiet, Ice Out

Ice out in my yard sneaks up slowly and mostly quietly.
I have two hand dug ponds.
They do not creak and crack like a large lake does.
The only sound is the slow drip of snow melting off the roof
and following the gutter that feeds the ponds.
Quiet, like the sound of snow melting into the frozen
ground.
Quiet, like the sound of sap in trees waking up to run up
the trunk.
Quiet, like the sound of the earth soaking up sun's rays
and water.
Quiet, as the earth wakes up from its frozen state.
Quiet, like the sound of grass twitching and lifting from its
winter solitude.
Quiet, like the sound of my soul waking to something new.
Quiet, like the sound of ice out.

***

Bill Herring
Minnetonka, MN

Resurrection

In the dark cocoon
Where the caterpillar dies
An angel is born.

Julie Babb
Damariscotta, ME

Evening Sail

Goodbye is such a lonely word
Filled with hope. Filled with loss—but we're not done yet,
Are we? Are we?
Longer nights stretch out before me;
Perhaps an apricot for dinner—nothing more....
Nothing more, nothing less than its sweet juice
Filling my mouth, wetting my cheeks with its tears.

Goodbye is such a lonely word
Filled with desperation. Filled with fear—but we're not done yet,
Are we? Are we?
Longer days stretch out before me;
Perhaps a walk on the beach—nothing more....
Nothing more, nothing less than the soft sand
Cradling my toes, bathing my feet with salt tears.

I have watched you drift away, day by day, hour by hour,
As you head for different shores, different climes
Places I cannot fathom where I cannot breathe the air.
I scan the sky line for glimpses, shadows of your sails—
But twilight comes upon me and I must leave.

Goodbye is such a lonely word.
But we're not done yet—are we?
Are we? Are we?

Charles Kaska
Heath Springs, SC

Postcard from Phinda

I knew the rifle's magazine was loaded with four rounds of Nitro Express in high caliber. It rested unobtrusively in the zippered case lashed to the hood of the Land Cruiser. I estimated that it would take our guide about 12 seconds to cover the distance from where he stood, unzip the case, chamber a round, acquire the target and squeeze off a shot. Unless his hands were shaking too much...

We had headed out on safari at first light on a chilly winter morning and within an hour discovered the carcass of a wildebeest that had been killed and mostly devoured during the night. Everyone exited the Cruiser to get a closer look, everyone except Shipo, our tracker, and me. He continued to search the gently waving grass with his high powered binoculars and when he turned he saw that I was glassing the opposite direction with my low powered compacts. "What you look for?" demanded Shipo, confused that I was not down with the others.

"I look for lion," I replied.

"Lion?" repeated Shipo. Then a knowing smile formed on his face: "Me too."

We both knew that the lion could be on his way back, perhaps with other members of his pride, to finish the meal. We did not want any of our people to be a second course. The muted colors of the winter foliage provide camouflage; the undulating grass masks movement. Knowing this does not cause fear, just the realization that in Phinda we are no longer the apex predator.

David Villano
Jefferson, ME

Forest Trail with Ocean Views

The protruded root
that breaks your stride
and the low-sweeping limb of oak
and the pine with twin trunks
of remarkable girth
(for a forest logged not so long ago)
and the mushroom cap
affixed to a rotted stump
and nibbled upon
the night before
and the angular wedge
of salted granite
three feet or so above mean high tide
from which you pause to drink
and scan the horizon
for the bobbing head of a seal
and then close your eyes to rest
before reversing your steps.

The return seems oddly faster
(and it is).
Your gait sturdy,
a seamless glide
through mottled forest,
less deference
to any new encounters
and more to the familiar ones
that lie beyond,
the lazy rhythm of discovery
giving way
to the steady cadence of expectation

(con't.)

David Villano
Jefferson, ME

for the signposts
you've made your own...
the oak, the rock, the root, the pine,
the stump with the mushroom
nibbled upon the night before.

***

Last Child at the Beach

The others drift away one by one
(sometimes in twos)
on bikes or in back seats,
or barefoot across fields and backyards
in the straightest line to dry cloths
and the crumbs
of salty snacks
stashed in a cupboard.

For an instant, by chance I'm sure,
he stands alone:
the day's laggard wrapped in a towel.

His pause is brief,
born less of reverence than practicality:
a missing sandal,
a far-flung shirt
or some small, buried bauble
of youthful distraction.

Whole again, he retreats,
indifferent to his plight,
shuffling unsteadily
through sand surprisingly cooler
than the early night air.

Sylvia Little-Sweat
Wingate, NC

A Still-Life Study

The abandoned house
slumps beneath its rusted tin
in still disarray.

Once yards were swept bare
by kin who pruned the broom straw,
kept geraniums.

Now weathered deep gray
porch planks creak, and sudden gusts
slam the screen door shut.

Day by day is marked
by sun and shade, rain or snow—
Time supplanting time.

Darkness falls each night
on vacant rooms that echo
distant songs of owls.

Inside, mice scamper,
and spiders weave their silken
webs across windows.

No one lives within.
Thus, who hangs holiday wreaths
on the old screen door?

Mary McClure
Jacksonville, OR

Pushing the River

Strapped into a neck brace in the ambulance, I couldn't stop asking questions. As the siren blared, I asked, "What's in that IV bag? You aren't giving me drugs, are you?" The EMT, Clara, smiled and assured me it was just saline solution.

"How are you feeling?" she asked, gently wiping blood from my face.

"Good. I'm good," I said, my heart bouncing in my chest, as they wheeled me into the Redding Trauma Center, into harsh fluorescent lights and shiny surfaces. I saw the neurosurgeon, all gowned-up, staring at me.

Oh, no, I thought, *they're going to drill a hole in my head.*

Little did I know that surgery was the least of it. This accident continues to challenge my identity at every turn, even a year later.

Leading up to the accident, I'd started a new chapter in my life, running a small care-giving business and writing children's books. These stories were inspired by observing my grandchildren play; two girls aged six and nine, whose imaginations are like rushing water: bubbly, exhilarating, and powerful.

A few days earlier, I'd driven to a mineral spa in northern California, where the sun filtered through tall pines, wood smoke rose above the sweat lodge, and the river galloped below. I'd come to enjoy the hot springs, one of the most powerful rejuvenators on earth. For hundreds of years, native people gathered on these lands. Each tribe brought their knowledge, medicine, and goods to trade and to share. Warriors left their weapons on the surrounding hills and all came together to celebrate. For me, this place was an earthly nirvana.

Growing up in the land of ten thousand lakes, I've found

Mary McClure
Jacksonville, OR

solace in the reflections of glimmering water. Rivers, especially, set my soul alight, with their sweeping energy, swirling eddies, and glistening rocky shores.

On the day of my accident, I had decided to take a walk along the riverbed and build a balance tower out of river rocks. I needed to pay homage to the water. I had been soaking my tired old body in the baths for two days, and getting massages in between. In other words, I was blissed out, not looking where I was going, when I slipped and fell off the path. I tumbled down a rocky embankment, head over heels. I came to a stop upside down. My neck was bending on its tender stem trying to support my trembling body. I couldn't breathe. I was waiting for my neck to break. I thought I was going to die.

When my neck miraculously didn't break, I slowly pushed myself over, gasping for breath. My right arm hung limply, numb and useless. Blood was streaming down my face from deep cuts, still stinging. Maybe it was the shock, but once I stood up, I didn't really feel that bad. I went into action, my mind whirring. Nobody was going to save me. I had to save myself. I've always been the family guardian, taking care of others. I'm a no-drama mama.

Stumbling up the muddy hill, I conjured my inner Superwoman, assessing the damage. I was too busy diagnosing myself to feel the pain. My racing brain was creating a no-nonsense to-do list.

Once in the emergency room, my hyper-vigilance kicked in. *I was aghast that the staff wanted to inject Lidocaine into my head given that I had a brain bleed and concussion. With blood flowing down my neck, I argued with the physician. Why put such a strong drug into such a traumatized area? We still didn't know if I needed brain surgery or not, did we? I refused the drugs and they sewed me up with a staple gun. In five seconds it was done.*

A week later, I sat in my physician's office sporting two trekker poles that allowed me to walk, barely. My right arm was bruised and hanging, my neck stiff and aching. Dr. Rosemary, an expressive bird-like woman, was my primary care doctor. She was direct in a warm, funny way. I have to say that I've made her jaw drop and eyes roll on more than one occasion.

Leaning forward in her chair, Dr. Rosemary patted my knee gently and informed me that I was lucky to be alive. "Most people your age probably wouldn't have survived that fall. Your Pilates classes paid off. Your physical flexibility saved you from a broken neck." She picked up my chart and examined it for moment. "You're looking at a 6- to 12-month recovery for the multiple head injuries you sustained."

I sat up a little straighter and announced, "Oh no, I'll be better in a few weeks."

I can handle this, I thought. Growing up, I was always the responsible one, the kid taking care of her alcoholic father. I have always been extremely resilient.

Dr. Rosemary sighed, reaching out to hug me, "Don't push the river. Let the current flow at its own pace."

Taking the disability bus home, I pondered what Dr. Rosemary had said. Was I trying to swim upstream? All I knew was that I had to find a new normal. A new way of being in the world while I healed.

My first lesson was the biggest shock: long-time friends I expected to help drifted away, while new ones stepped up to take their places. In a demanding world, where people struggle to survive, my old friends didn't want to see their own frail existence mirrored in me. Marisol, however, was different. Before the accident, Marisol and I worked as care-givers at the local hospice. Although much younger than me, she sought out a friendship, inviting me to a family picnic in the park. I met her daughters and grandchildren. Over watermelon, Marisol told me, she never knew what "play" was until watching her grandchildren. She had been the eldest of nine, always the mother, never the child. I knew something about that, serving as my father's care-taker, calling the bars when he forgot to come home, running to the neighbors when he got violent, and helping my mother to keep a lid on things.

Marisol was my savior, coming once a week to help me clean and run errands. She'd bring me bags of homemade cookies, love, and encouragement. I learned what the patient feels towards the caregiver. One is so vulnerable to the world when disabled. I had to trust Marisol completely, with every detail of my life. I gained a new respect for what my patients endowed me with.

My second lesson was a revelation. I wasn't Superwoman. I wasn't healing on my schedule, no matter how hard I pushed that river. Eight months after the accident, in Dr. Rosemary's office, I announced that I was going to Los Angeles to visit my friends and have some fun. She told me: "It's too soon, Mary. What you're not looking at is how tiring flying is. You won't be in your own place. You'll be much more active and all these things can be detrimental to your healing process."

It took me days and days to let go of my plans. My mind kept trying to find ways to get to Los Angeles despite her advice. How can I pull this plan off? How can I swim upstream?

After a long day of doctors' visits and physical therapy, with my head pounding and my balance giving way to dizziness, I just realized that she was right and I had to listen to her. I didn't want to believe I was still so vulnerable, so needy. I wanted to be the responsible one and get back to my old life again. But I couldn't. Not yet. And still now not yet. But I've learned to be in the moment, to watch the stream flow, and to honor my body and my new-found friends.

P. C. Moorehead
North Lake, WI

The Ecology of Life

I heard the thousandth bird
in the faraway earth
sing its last song,
and I cried,

cried for the lost bird,
cried for the lost earth,
cried for the lost life
of us all.

The thousandth bird sang,
and I listened,
listened to its lost voice
rising over the lost land.

Will it survive?
I do not know.
Will I survive?
I do not know.

Lost bird,
lost earth,
lost song,
lost me.

Rebecca Brooks
Topsham, ME

Found

The anticipated visit and rueful footfalls
among my painted trees
are lonesome reminders
of fair-weather company.

One by one, white pine and birch
will point you north,
as verdant moss
clings to skyward watchmen.
Mother Nature's Compass Rose
will lead you down the Devil's Back,
while searching osprey soar above,
regal on the wind.

What brings you here amid my rugged veins?
Life unbroken
with every intertwining quiet pulse.
Have you forgotten the fragile lichen,
who cling to the keeper of my passage?
Can you remember the smell of Quahog Bay
and her white lilies in full bloom?

Will you tarry
and rediscover our connection?
I fear your time with me is evanescent,
but I remain steadfast
long after your footprints wane.

Rosalie Ann Lopresto
Rye, NH

Escape to My Cottage in Maine

For decades toward the end of spring I would hear people say, "I am going up to camp" or "I am going up to the cottage." I smiled, yet would feel this sense of yearning to know more without prying. Weekend after weekend I would drag my husband all over the state of Maine until he started feeling what I was feeling. It was contagious: the brisk air, miles of rocky untouched coastline, formidable mountains and picturesque landscape. We discovered lovely, old Maine lake cottages with envious views, charming towns with understated elegance and shops with local Maine fare. We explored trails by bike and foot uncovering blueberries, streams, waterfalls and vistas beyond.

How I became quickly mesmerized in the moment. The idea that one can place a pre-made wooden sign on the outside of a shop that reads, "gone fishing...gone hiking...gone skiing...gone to the lake...gone what-ever" without any time of return. Just imagine the ability to do that. The possibility of actually doing that on one's perceived perfect juncture in time on a pristine sunny day or an idyllic winter day without any hesitation. Still in reverie? Envision, as I have, acquiring a cottage or cabin and the excitement of bestowing novel memories to future generations of one's precious and selfish time in Maine.

Maine became a place for inspiration without presumption. The trips to the mountains, islands and lakes made me wonder about myself. I felt captivated by the beauty that surrounded me which was as intense as a lover's hug. The feeling of ennui subsided to be quickly replaced by intense curiosity and nature's magnificence. Carpe diem was the expectation, and contemplation became subservient. Our sojourns in Maine brought a compelling desire for a place of our own.

Rosalie Ann Lopresto
Rye, NH

After a glorious sunrise late summer, I found myself in a trance-like state while sitting on a natural, jutting ledge overlooking the reflective lake. The trance was broken with the sound of the loon's wail. Time passed without concern. I got into my kayak and felt a part of the lake. I slowly paddled toward the loons to become acquainted. I headed to the nearby island, secured the kayak and enjoyed a refreshing swim in the spring-fed water. I did not feel hurried. The familiar bearded flinty old man paddled by with his hunter green LL Bean canoe as he does each morning. Without faltering, I continued on my day's journey of reflection, introspection and mindfulness: the feeling of my transformation becoming part of the lake's DNA. I deeply inhaled and thought about the "6 Rs" from Joan Anderson's book, *A Weekend to Change Your Life*—retreat, repair, retrieve, regroup, regenerate and return.

I paddled all day long not concerned about time nor obligation. I unearthed a pulchritude inspired by the glory and scents around me. I felt a sense of freedom that I did not think was actually real. Was I still daydreaming? I followed the star's orbit and loon's call until the jaw-dropping galaxy lit up the sky—the Milky Way. It was magical. Truly, I did not want this day to end.

Each sunrise at the lake unleashes the anticipation of nature's itinerary. The breathtaking allure of the water and its surroundings conveys the sense of calmness that I was seeking and will continue to seek. What shall this day bring? Oh how I must never sleep in! Johann Wolfgang von Goethe was right when he said, "Nothing is worth more than this day. You cannot relive yesterday." This is now my decade to finally say, "I am heading north to my cottage in Maine."

Sally Belenardo
Branford, CT

"FIFI" RENAMED: "ALLUCE" Italian—Al (to), Luce (light) *pronounced AL-LOO-CHAY*

The miniature poodle looks like a pink dog,
her black coat shaved off without care,
dried blood on scrapes and cuts in her skin.

Now no one can tell she was matted with filth,
could hardly move her hind end,
had to drag herself along.

Infested with whipworms,
her thin body is exposed. It hurts to walk,
gait stilted by nails grown so long

they curl sideways under her paws.
She has spent thirteen years confined
in the squalid cellar of a vacant house,

bearing puppies for sale.
She isn't saved in time to see her new life very well,
her dark eyes nearly sightless,

though she discerns light from darkness,
gets around table and chair legs,
knows where her food is set down,

finds her soft bed on the floor,
navigates the step from kitchen to porch,
breathes fresh air, feels the sun,

and, guided by harness and leash,
she walks in the yard's grass and clover,
knowing this is home, forever.

Janet Dorman
Falmouth, ME

Because I Love You, I Eat the Brazil Nuts

Because I love you, I eat the Brazil nuts.

You dislike them.
        Intensely.
        Loudly.
        Unreasonably.
You claim they take up space in the can of Deluxe Mixed
        Nuts.
"What is so deluxe," you sneer, "about a Brazil nut?"

A character in a daily comic strip states
that Brazil nuts are the Detroit Lions of the nut world.
You would agree.
        Intensely.
        Mockingly.
        Laughingly.

But because I love you, I eat the Brazil nuts.

Do I eat them as a sacrificial offering of love,
        reverently placed on the altar that is
        the coffee table that holds our drinks?

Do I eat them because I know they offend your taste buds,
        and I would spare you any offense, laying down
        my tongue as Sir Walter lay down his cloak for a
                queen?

Or do I eat them to pre-empt your complaining?
        Not so noble perhaps,
                but...
                maybe...

Janet Dorman
Falmouth, ME

I eat them because I like them
        and
        because
        I secretly root for the Detroit Lions.

***

Robert B. Moreland
Pleasant Prairie, WI

Enough

When life's stresses come
the immediate replacing the important,
I want to take you to the great lake at sunset,
pinkness fading to dusky twilight
with the innocence of that first star
appearing hesitant, then bright.

I would be so alone without you here;
your stubborn intelligence,
a playground sense of justice
assuring me regardless, that it will be alright.

In the stillness with waves lapping the shore,
I would take your hand, embrace and watch
the evening constellations pepper the sky,
our known universe only as far as we can see.

How hard it is to believe in things unseen!
But I know your love and your loyalty.
I do not have any of the answers
to so many questions. But in the darkness,
your warmth next to me is enough.

Georgette Carignan
Limerick, ME

Spiral

It slithers
Unbidden,
Into our souls and psyche.
Tentacles
Cling
Capturing our thoughts.
Fearful thoughts.
Baseless thoughts,
Sometimes.

It burrows
Deep into our cortex,
To nest.
To stay.
To survive.
Unrelenting
In its goals.

When light
Attempts to enter,
We cower,
Uncomfortable in its
Brightness.
Who are we to deserve
Light?

Imperfect beings
That we are
We cling to what we know,
And watch our happiness
Recede.

Ilga Winicov Harrington
Falmouth, ME

Aunt Hilda

We are standing at the Lufthansa gate and my head is whirling in turmoil, oblivious of the airport noise and bustle of crowds. The voice from yesterday's phone call keeps repeating in my head.

"I'm Dr. Johannes from the St. Agnes Krankenhaus in Kőln. Your aunt is my patient and asked me to call you. I'm afraid I have bad news. We discovered that her cancer has spread so extensively that she is likely to have only a short time left." His voice was gentle with a slight German accent.

In short order we were able to get tickets for a flight to Germany, rearrange our busy schedules and now a day later, my husband and I are on our way. Aunt Hilda, my mother's younger sister had been a second mother to me all my life. Although we now lived an ocean apart, the connection had been kept strong by frequent letters, hers with artistic doodles in the borders and the attention of a calligrapher's hand compared to my less elegant scribblings. We had visited on both sides of the ocean and my husband had fondly nicknamed her his *Auntie Mame* for her exuberance to life was more than equal to that of the famed stage character. She seemed indomitable.

***

Hilda was more than an aunt. She was someone who would safely answer questions by a child, that could not be asked the rest of the adults in my world. She was also an artist, the black sheep of the family and the most romantic person I have ever known. Her self-portrait from the 1930's still holds that image as it shows her sitting on a red velvet stool, in front of dark red silk hangings, wearing a white filmy evening dress that reveals crossed shapely legs. She is leaning forward, chin resting on one palm of her hand assessing the viewer with a curious and slightly critical gaze. Her off shoulder dress is bordered all around in soft and light white fur. My practical mother thought it frivolous.

Aunt Hilda's greatest pleasures were people she loved, and painting. She had attended the Academy of Art in Riga, Latvia, but found some of the rules too constricting. Her portraits were incredibly insightful, infused by the person's mood and character, and later in life she made a living as a painter of portraits and other beautiful paintings. After the German occupation of Latvia in 1941 she worked in the city hospital as a practical nurse, mostly in wards of injured soldiers. She was a gentle and sympathetic nurse to those young men who had lost an arm or leg and will to go on. She was fluent in German, Latvian and Russian, as were most Latvians of her generation and she also spoke French. She would write letters home for the soldiers and sometimes she would cheer them by drawing sketches of them or animals. During those years she met Karl, a tailor conscript to the German army, who was stationed in Riga. It was love at first sight, but since he was part of the occupying army, many in her family disapproved.

As the second wave of WWII swept over Latvia, families lost track of each other routinely and so did we of Aunt Hilda. In the aftermath of the war we ended up in Würzburg Germany. Eventually my mother found that Aunt Hilda had been caught in the Russian Zone at the time of Germany's partition between East and West and we feared for her life.

But then, in early spring of 1946, a tall gaunt woman with sunken eyes and sallow cheeks arrived at the gates of Central Displaced Persons (DP) camp in Würzburg. Someone directed her to us in a corner of the communal room on the second floor in building #5.

My mother took one look and screamed: "Oh my God, Hilda" and threw her arms around the gaunt woman.

My mother's younger sister had escaped the Russian

Zone and had found us in Würzburg. She was ill, she had been starving, but she had found us. We hugged and cried and for a short time we simply forgot the stiff distance and serious demeanor of people with Northern European origins. We listened with amazement to her story of determined perseverance during the last year.

She had been caught in the Russian Zone and her language skills enabled her to become a translator in administrative offices and thus avoid persecution. But then she became ill and was diagnosed with advanced cervical cancer. She had surgery followed by extensive radiation treatments, but the prognosis remained bad. She had been given a few months to live.

Aunt Hilda knew we had made it to Würzburg and decided that she did not want to die alone. So, she gathered what money she had and proceeded to escape East Germany to the American Zone. The worst she claimed was walking through a section of the woods near the border at night, guided by someone local, all the time expecting to be caught or shot by the Russian border patrol. In her weakened state, it was agony. According to her, when they finally made it to a safe area and her guide left to return, she just lay down on the forest moss and howled with a fist in her mouth in order not to make any noise. She had expected to die that night and even now carried with her the death sentence from the East German doctors.

In the DP camp she was promptly seen by doctors, who to everyone's surprise and joy found that although she had a lot of scar tissue from the radiation, there seemed to be no further signs of cancer. Aunt Hilda would find a new life stretching before her to be filled with laughter and tears for another 40 plus years.

She would paint and write me wonderful letters in her calligraphic script and continue to treat me as the daughter she never had. Years later she would come to visit me in America and amuse my two sons in French, since she spoke

Ilga Winicov Harrington
Falmouth, ME

no English, and French was the only foreign language the boys had learned in school. Most of all, she continued to provide me with unstructured form of mothering that actually approved of *style* for *appearances* and gave me glimpses into the adult world that were not as straight-laced as those of my strict and practical mother.

While still in the DP camp, she was able to contact her great love Karl Garbe, who with the dissolution of the German army had returned to Kőln. They married and the rest of her life was spent in Kőln.

Years later Aunt Hilda would gently remind me of my arrogant eleven-year self on that parting.

"I won't have you as a proper aunt anymore, if you marry a German," I pronounced even while sobbing my goodbye in her arms. "You will leave and I'll never see you again."

Fortunately, neither she nor Uncle Karl put much stock in these juvenile theatrics. They invited me to visit them a couple of years later, before we emigrated to America from Germany.

That was a strange and wonderful visit, as they were the only extended family I had left. Uncle Karl had a new tailor shop in their apartment and was doing well, so that they sent me a train ticket to come and visit them. By today's standards it may sound surprising to put a thirteen-year-old girl alone for a long day's ride on a train in Würzburg, Southern Germany to be met by an aunt and uncle in Kőln, Northern Germany. Strange as it seems now, life then appeared more secure.

The main train station in Kőln in 1948 was minimally reconstructed after the war. I vividly remember coming out of the station and facing a huge empty square. Bombed out devastation was still everywhere. For blocks, in all directions one could see only rubble and an occasional wall or two still standing like skeletons overlooking a wasteland.

In the midst of all this desolation stood a stark miracle across the square. It was dark and covered with black soot, but its spires thrust their centuries proud and majestic silhouettes against the white tufted blue sky. The Dom Cathedral had survived as a witness to Allied precision bombing, with only one back corner slightly damaged in the midst of all the backdrop of devastation. Interestingly, one of the other landmarks that survived in central Kőln was a fragment of an ancient wall from the Middle Ages, that depicts the old story of *The Shoemaker and the Elves* telling of the elves who came to do the shoemaker's work at night. Probably no miracles of precision bombing were involved there, though other magic has never been disproved.

***

Our drive from Frankfurt to Kőln was uneventful, but quiet. My husband was concentrating on the high-speed traffic on the Autobahn and I was lost in memories. We stopped at a florist's shop and bought red roses and found the hospital on a quiet side street. We were directed to her room and entered it with trepidation of what we would find. The brightness of the long room did not obscure the fact that it was a women's ward, with six beds aligned against the wall. The nurse pointed to a bed in the center, where Aunt Hilda was asleep on her side. Her pale face was restful in sleep, but the gaunt sunken cheeks and deep dark circles under her eyes testified to her suffering.

Her eyes opened slowly and an instant smile lit her face: *Mīļo meit*! she whispered in Latvian as usual calling me her *dear daughter.*

"You came, I knew you would," she continued and reached for my hand as I leaned down to kiss her whisper-thin cheek. My throat was so tight, for a moment I could say nothing while holding her hand.

"Yes, we both came," I choked out in a raspy voice and pointed to my husband.

But Aunt Hilda would have no tearful talk. She painfully

Ilga Winicov Harrington
Falmouth, ME

sat up, fluffed up her dark curls and turned to my husband.

"Ja, du bist ein gutes Mann, bestimmt," she switched to German, a language he also understood. Aunt Hilda spoke no English. But then the conversation reverted to Latvian, since my German had seriously slipped during the years and we wanted privacy. She quietly told me that she had not paid attention to a lump in her breast for some time, but had finally come to the hospital a couple of weeks ago, when the pain became so bad she no longer could do her daily marketing. There had been tests and thankfully pills for the pain. In one breath she acknowledged that the cancer had spread everywhere and with another breath she talked about going back to her little apartment. *This was all going to be very difficult*!

Amazingly, even in the hospital she had continued to sketch the doctors, nurses and the flowers that were brought to the patients in the ward. She had given the portraits away, but her notebook still held sketches of the various flowers. As we talked, bits of information came out in short bursts. Her landlord had come and visited her with his wife. Her stepsons had not spoken to her in years. She loved her red roses and no, she did not need anything. Her landlord would take care of everything that needed doing when *this* was over. An admission, but she refused to pursue details.

Suddenly, she thought she would like to go out from the hospital for an outing and the nurse was encouraging.

"It will give her a different focus," she said quietly and added, "she has been depressed the last few days."

As we helped her dress, we could see how difficult it had become for Aunt Hilda to move. A small pill was brought to keep her pain at bay and we wheeled her out in a wheelchair to the back seat of our car. The nurse made her comfortable with several pillows and we were off on a bizarre adventure for someone who insisted on being extraordinary to the end.

She wanted to be taken to some of her favorite places in downtown Kőln around the Dom Cathedral square, along the river Rhein and through some of the non-pedestrian shopping streets. She was a frustrating navigator from the back seat in both Latvian and German. Though she had walked and shopped on these streets for years, the view from the car seemed confusing.

"Uz augšu" ("up above"—Latvian), she kept insisting on her old familiar route. I was ashamed to admit after several tense exchanges to almost losing my temper after circling a couple of blocks several times.

"Grade aus" ("straight ahead"—German) finally solved the dilemma. Amazingly, we managed with my husband driving and my translations, both of us running on adrenalin and very little sleep.

I was twice as ashamed when we finally arrived at her destination. It was her favorite art supply store. We went in and the owner was most solicitous of his long-time customer. After a rapid-fire consultation in German, some brushes were brought out, ones that she preferred to use for her pastel work. *Yes, this was pure denial! But, we bought her those brushes.*

After the art store we backtracked to a small street behind the Dom and went for an early supper in a quiet small restaurant. It was dark paneled and dim, with the usual beer steins on the mantle. The stone arches had been reconstructed after the war and it appeared as if the white tablecloths had gleamed there for a hundred years, the red-capped lights on each table giving a secure arc of personal lighted space. We ordered veal and Aunt Hilda ordered chicken in an elegant sauce. All went well, until she tasted the potatoes, which had been prepared in a modern way, meaning "not cooked to death." Aunt Hilda pronounced them undercooked and sent them back. The waiter kept a straight face and politely made the necessary adjustments. It provided badly needed comic relief. Aunt Hilda would remain indomitable until the end.

The next day was harder. We could only stay three days

Ilga Winicov Harrington
Falmouth, ME

in Germany and would have to leave early the next morning. We spent the morning at the hospital and another outing was planned for the afternoon. The skies had clouded up and it started to rain intermittently, but Aunt Hilda was ready to go in her black raincoat. Where this time?

"I want to visit the cemetery. *Mein Mann is da und auch mein Schwiegervater.*"

Her deceased husband would always be *mein Mann* and her father-in-law had been very dear to her, since he had been the one person who had accepted her when she became part of Uncle Karl's family upon marriage. So, we went to the cemetery.

We had visited the burial plot previously, but one could not drive inside the main gate. We stopped at the gatehouse and it started to rain seriously. The gatekeeper was a kind old man and offered us the use of a wheelchair, kept for elderly visitors. He even lent us a large umbrella. My husband would stay with the car and I would find the gravesites with Aunt Hilda despite the now pouring rain.

We walked slowly, since I was both pushing the wheelchair on the gravelly walkways and balancing the umbrella above us. The rain was coming down steadily and in the dreary light under the tree-lined walks even the spring flowers looked dreary. The umbrella was black, her coat was black, our mood was black. I can't remember another instance when the whole world seemed as dark as that walk in the cemetery.

At one point she said, "I knew you would understand" and no more.

We finally stopped at a low boxwood-bordered enclosure marked with a tan stone and the family name GARBE. She leaned forward, hands clasped, and I could see a world of loss and misery in her face. I took a few steps back, on the pretext of going to look at a nearby monument and left her with the umbrella for a few minutes. *If she was going to be brave, I certainly could not let her see me cry.* It was starting

Ilga Winicov Harrington
Falmouth, ME

to rain harder, so I went back to the grave site with Aunt Hilda and the umbrella.

As I came closer, I could hear her talking in German, more correctly, imploring: "Hilfe, mir, hilfe mir...." she was calling to her dead husband.

I laid a hand on her shoulder.

She grasped my hand, "We will be together again. Let's get back to the car; we are both getting soaked."

Back at the hospital it was easy to see that the outing had been too much for her. The little pills were wearing off and she would take a deep breath every now and then as the pain assaulted her. We got her back in bed and the nurse came with another dose of medicine.

The ward was being closed for the evening and we had to leave. We hugged and held close for a long time. She insisted I take a picture of a lily she had sketched with colored pencils for my oldest son. As I reached the door, she called me back and insisted I take her sketchbook as well.

Finally leaving, she said, "Auf wiedersehen."

And I answered in Latvian, "Uz redzi." Both of us knowing that it would not be in "this lifetime."

The following day, after we had arrived home, the call came from Germany. She had taken her last breath as we crossed the ocean. *Hilfe mir.* The help she had fervently cried out for at the cemetery, freedom from her stoic fight with pain, had come at last. Peace.

Stacie Santillo
York, PA

Golden Hour

Water purls beneath me
deadwood trees cathedral
to my daughter's voice—a canticle
of it's beautiful here.

Bowing in your baptistery
I am a profligate sinner,
treading upon parched wildflowers
bereft of birdsong, stalking peace
among holy beasts burdened
by the weight of the wanton,
those unmoved by your majesty,
their eyes scorched from traveling
too close to the sun. I am a serial
interloper watching you—
the white-winged huntress—
aigrettes glistening like Io dust
from Jupiter's rings.

Together, we are like
the golden hour, dwindling

waiting

in the flare of the sun
like life between breaths.

waiting

in the dusk amidst
death and deliverance.

Jean Biegun
Davis, CA

Under Spring Leaves

The undersides of leaves
for some reason

lift ordinary days.
Could be their just-born

whispery colors or their lacy
feathering veins. So very much

to wonder about, to touch
outside the backyard door.

And here is that stand-up
comedian of a squirrel again

inching up the slippery pole
for the bird feeder and again

slowly slipping back down,
that same what-the-heck look

of puzzlement on its face,
making me want to stay out

under leaves this whole day
for the wonder, the fun of it all.

Steve Troyanovich
Florence, NJ

kingdom of shadows

and I hold your picture
deep inside my heart
—Jackie Leven

laboring sunward
shadows tumble
through my hands...
seeking your touch
time remains
a long lonely picture
i cannot understand

***

hyperborean blues

in the morning
without ever meeting
our lips fade into memories
of trembling snowflakes
and butterfly wings...

somewhere the fragrance
of your hair
fills nocturnal orchards
while our embrace mingles
with the soft caress
of a violin wind...

Kaye Nelson Ratliff
Wadesboro, NC

Come Ye Thankful People, Come

Julie raises her hand to cradle her aching head even as she becomes aware of the rising gorge in her stomach. Looking around, she sees that she hasn't made it home again this morning, that she's still on the couch where she passed out last night at someone's apartment. Along with her physical pain, she feels a sense of bleakness and shame. She's overwhelmed by feelings of helplessness and hopelessness, knowing down deep in her soul that she's lost. Lost to her former self, lost to her present, lost to her future.

It happened slowly after her parents died. Her older brother and sister were able to move on, but Julie just couldn't find a way forward. The alcohol and pot seemed to numb the gaping hole in her soul for a while, but recently numbness has turned into a new kind of pain.

Julie slowly gets herself off the couch and to the bathroom where she throws water on her face and drinks from the tap to cool her parched mouth. She puts toothpaste on her finger and attempts to finger-brush her teeth which feel coated in flannel. Having performed these minor ablutions, she creeps past the other sleeping forms in the living room, past empty cans and bottles and reeking ashtrays, past small mirrors lightly coated in a white powder, to the door where she exits into the second floor hall. At the bottom of the stairs, she walks out into a glorious late autumn morning, the sun shining brightly in a brilliant blue sky, and suddenly remembers that it's Thanksgiving Day.

As she walks along a sidewalk filled with filthy litter and vibrant leaves, she passes a church and hears the sound of music wafting from the sanctuary. The congregants are singing "Come Ye Thankful People, Come," and Julie's heart is filled with the exquisite pain of remembering the Thanksgivings of her youth, before the tragedy that wrecked her life. She remembers attending church with her family, Mother being anxious that the turkey and dressing were moist, Daddy and Brother Jim watching football while the girls help their mother in the kitchen.

God, if you'll give me a second chance, I'll try hard to change, I'll go to rehab, AA meetings, church, whatever it takes to get clean and sober and back to a decent life. Please, God, a second chance, please. Julie is so overwhelmed by regret and sorrow as she crosses the street against the light, she fails to see the car coming through the intersection, cannot hear the screech of brakes as it hits her and she sails into the air.

"Hello, are you awake? I'm Dr. Harris, the hospitalist, and this is Dr. Drake, the orthopedic surgeon who operated on you. Can you tell us your name?"

Julie opens her eyes and the two men come into focus. "I'm Julie Martin," she mumbles.

"Do you know where you are?"

Feelings of pain shoot through her body as she answers, "Uh, I guess I'm in the hospital. What's happened?"

"You were hit by a car and suffered several injuries, including a compound fracture of your right leg, a cracked left elbow, and a concussion," Dr. Harris explains. "Frankly, Julie, you're lucky to be alive, and lucky that you're not more injured than you are."

Dr. Drake picks up the narrative. "You'll be in the hospital for several days, maybe weeks. We'll need to monitor you for blood clots or other complications. When you are stabilized, we'll move you to the step-down unit for rehab until you're able to return home on your own. Any questions?"

Julie is overwhelmed by all this information. She merely says, "I don't remember anything except passing a church, then crossing the street."

"Well, your blood alcohol was elevated and you tested positive for THC, so I suppose you may have been somewhat impaired at the time of your accident. Plus, the concussion.

A social worker will be around to follow up on any additional needs you have," Dr. Harris replies.

"And we'll keep you as comfortable as possible with pain management," Dr. Drake adds.

Julie cringes, wondering what these doctors must think of her.

The following day a social worker does appear. "Hi, Julie. My name is Pamela Ellis. I'm the hospital social worker, and I'll be helping plan for your non-medical needs and your discharge and follow-up. First, I noticed you had no next-of-kin or emergency contact information listed. Is there someone I can contact for you?"

"No," Julie responds. "There's no one who would care. But I guess you should call my employer. I work at the Old Stage Café. The owner is Hank McIver."

"I'll be glad to do that, Julie. Are you sure there's no one else? A young minister has been coming by and checking on you. In fact, he sat in the surgical waiting room until we could assure him that you came through the surgery okay. But we really couldn't tell him anything without your consent."

"Minister? I don't have a minister."

"Well, he sure acts like your minister, and he's here now if you'd like to see him."

"I guess it's okay. I'll see him if he wants to come in." Julie is curious as to why this minister has been so concerned about her.

A man about 30 years old, wearing a black shirt and jacket with a white clerical collar enters her room. He smiles. "Hi, Julie. I'm Reverend Mike Boyce from the First Presbyterian Church on Madison Avenue. I'm glad to see you made it through your accident."

"How did you know I was hurt? Was it in the paper or something? Are you the hospital chaplain?"

"No, I'm the minister at the church near where you were hit. We were just finishing up the Thanksgiving service when we heard the crash. Then the sirens came screaming by. I came to the hospital to see if I could help in any way."

"But why? You don't know me."

"No, I don't know you. But sometimes people need a minister when bad things happen: someone to care, someone to pray for them."

"Thanks, I guess. I don't go to church anywhere, so I don't have a minister." *Or anyone else,* Julie thinks. "I remember hearing the music coming from your church just before I started across the street. It made me think of Thanksgivings I used to have." Julie sighs as she thinks back to that day and what was going through her mind. She laughs softly. "I guess that's what I was doing instead of paying attention to the traffic."

"Is it okay with you if I kind of be your minister while you're recuperating?"

"Yeah, I would like that. It's been a long time since I was in a church. I used to go when my parents were alive. They died when I was twelve."

"Your parents are deceased? Do you have other family?"

"An older brother and sister. But they don't live anywhere near here, and we don't keep in touch."

"May I ask why?"

"My parents died in a car crash. It was my fault."

"Oh? How is that?"

"I was fighting with my brother in the back seat and Dad reached back to stop me and lost control of the car. They were killed, but my brother and I survived."

"So, you've blamed yourself all these years. You were just a kid, Julie. Sometimes kids misbehave and sometimes they fight with their siblings. That's pretty normal stuff."

"But it killed my parents. It was my fault."

"No, Julie. It was an accident, not anyone's fault."

"Oh yeah? It was my fault then, and it was my fault yesterday when I stepped in the road in front of that car."

"Just another accident, Julie."

Kaye Nelson Ratliff
Wadesboro, NC

"I just want to rest now." All this talk is bringing up pain that had nothing to do with her injuries, and Julie desperately wants meds and to be numb.

"Okay, I'll leave you alone now, but may I pray with you first?" Julie consents, and Reverend Boyce prays. "Lord, give Julie peace and relief from all the pain she is suffering. And most of all, Lord, help Julie forgive herself, even as you have forgiven her. Amen."

Over the next several weeks Julie begins to mend. She goes to the rehab unit for therapy until she is able to walk with a walker and walking cast. During that time she receives many visits from Reverend Boyce and her coworkers from the café. A few days before Julie is scheduled to be discharged, Helen, an older waitress, comes by.

"I've got some good news, Julie," Helen says. "We've had a special tip jar at work for you. The customers have been real concerned about you and have been fillin' that jar up every day. We've collected enough to pay your rent for the next month or so, until you're able to come back to work. Hank's holdin' your job for you, too. We've all really missed you. And we've all been prayin' for you."

"Oh, Helen, how can I ever thank all of you? I don't deserve this, but I really do appreciate what you've done."

"Honey, you'd do the same for us. And you know that cute preacher from the Presbyterian Church? He's been coming in for lunch nearly every day. He has taken a real interest in you, Julie, and he keeps us up to date on how you're doin'. He's got a lot of his members comin' in, too. Why, Julie, you've been good for business!" Helen laughs and slaps her knee. "You just keep doin' good and you'll be back in no time at all."

The day for discharge finally comes. As Julie is preparing to leave, Reverend Boyce arrives. "I've come to give you a ride home if that's okay with you."

"That's very kind, Reverend Boyce. You've been a good friend to me during this ordeal. And spending all this time in the hospital, I've detoxed off alcohol and pot, and I can think more clearly. They've even made sure I'm off all pain meds, so I don't get hooked on those."

"That's wonderful, Julie. You know what they say, 'It's an ill wind that blows no good.' "

"Well, that's one way to look at all this. Seriously, though, getting sober, and your talking to me have helped me deal with my parents' death and my part in it. I'm still working on it, but I'm beginning to see that it may not have been altogether my fault."

"We have an AA group that meets at the church several nights a week. You might want to think about attending."

"I'm planning on it. I made God a promise to do just that."

***

Two years after her accident, Julie is asked to be the speaker and tell her story at an AA meeting.

"Hello, my name is Julie and I'm an alcoholic."

"Hello, Julie," the group responds.

"Two years ago, my life was a mess. I was drinking and drugging and barely hanging on. On Thanksgiving Day as I was crossing the street, I asked God for a second chance, and wow! Did he ever give me one!"

Andrea Hill
Jonesboro, ME

Steamers

A silver sliver grows on earth's brow,
lights the bay's brown back,
climbs into shore bound skiffs,
weathered clapboard capes and over wooden sloop bows.
It paints pearl white the grey mud flats that
surface in the salty air filled with
echoes of clammers' calls
with buckets, rakes, rollers, oars they prepare.

Tide falls around fertile middle ground,
dinghies are beached or anchored,
on per pound prices,
diggers move in boot sucking ooze
with sore backs that claw and twist
like yellow-billed gulls who
pluck clams to crack on pink rock cliffs.

Calloused palms crack, shoulders burn,
wind rises, turns south,
brings milky cirrus clouds in
to crowd the sun.
Its lemon glow behind pine and fir
wields shadows over the bay,
splits a coming sea
into dark and day.

Kedge lines grow taut,
dories sway then float.
Plastic totes full of soft-shells stowed,
worn outboards start hard,
some rakers row ashore, but
their footprints remain
to trace once more.

Bill Herring
Minnetonka, MN

A Lakeside Lunch

—for Sharon & Sean

I wonder what they're discussing
lakeside on this Minnetonka
Mother's Day afternoon.
Politics? They do that a lot.
The upcoming baseball season
or the recent NFL draft? Done that, too.
Is he telling her about his
new position with the Minnesota DFL?
Or could she be asking, "So,
who have you been seeing lately?"
Yes, even the best of moms are known
to cross the sacred line.

This is the continuation
of a lifelong dialogue that began
with a mocking bird lullaby
and baby babble that would someday
turn to simple words that would someday
come together in simple sentences,
soon compounded with adjectives
and adverbs, prepositions,
conjunctions and interjections.
Then restrictive and non-restrictive
clauses, and every so often
a dangling participle.
All the necessary linguistics needed
to carry on pleasant conversations
about politics, Major League Baseball,
the NFL draft, his new position with the DFL
while enjoying a lakeside lunch
on a Minnetonka Mother's Day afternoon.

Mary Ann Bedwell
Grants, NM

No Rain Falls

How can you say there is no spirit if you have never sat with a dying person and watched it leave the body? What does it look like, you ask? It looks like rain looks when it stops raining.

"And what does that look like?" asks the visiting Martian. And the cynic tries to answer.

"There is no more rain," he says. "No rain falls, the air is clear, things no longer get wet, the gutters cease to run and the pavement dries up."

"You say 'no rain' falls. And what is this mysterious 'no rain' that no longer falls?"

"But there is no rain, there is nothing to see or hear or taste or smell, nothing to act upon the environment! It is simply the rain was there and now it is not. In its absence, there is no rain. It is simply something that I know was there, that was apparent both by its presence and by its effects, and now is no more. Outside, there is no rain."

"Ah," said the Martian, "it is like the human spirit. We can only recognize its presence by its absence."

***

Sylvia Little-Sweat
Wingate, NC

Wisteria

In riotous Spring
Wisteria vines climb trees
Like school boys—just freed.

Cordula Mathias
Trevett, ME

So Many Questions

What Are Gulls?

Seabirds gliding elegantly
Overhead, glittering
Silvery in the reflecting
Sun

Or persons who are
Fooled or deceived?

Where does the adjective
Come from?
Is the pejorative
Gullible, a back-formation
From gullibility?

The phenomenon is
Ancient, think of the Trojan Horse
Or Samson in the Book of Judges

Yet the word "gullible" doesn't
Turn up in the American
Dictionary of the English Language
Until 1830

And here we are today
Hopelessly gullible, indulging
In what ifs and wishful
Thinking, at a time when
Self-preservation should long
Have kicked in.

Peggy Trojan
Brule, WI

Swimming Hole, 1942

We swam in the Brule
down by the park
as it rippled through town
on the way to Lake Superior.
Spring fed, frigid year-round.
Big boys cannonballed
from the bridge.
We girls, in our bikinis
and winter white skin,
waded in to our waists,
ducked under and hurried out,
shrieking for our towels.
Nancy, on the bank, yelled,
"Virginia, if you go into that whirlpool
and drown, Mother will never let
you come swimming again."

Published in *Ariel* 2021

***

Sally Belenardo
Branford, CT

Unfair

The musician was
charged with perjury because
he played the lyre.

Sylvia Little-Sweat
Wingate, NC

Indigo

At twilight
she wonders
what happened
to the light
what made her days
as thin as her skin
so faintly traced
in blue
where she had misplaced
her better self
like a letter or a key
and needed help to find it
when the cost of her loss
seemed too deep and slow
to fathom,
let alone let go
how in her pain
she was trapped like a wasp
behind the glass
shut tight.

what she wonders
at night
is what to do
with the dark.

Judy Driscoll Winchenbaugh
Rockland, ME

The Letters

Theresa reaches for the stack of love letters bound with a brittle rubber band. The letters have been in her nightstand for over fifty years, since the day her husband's fighter jet was shot down over the jungles of Vietnam. Henry's body was never found and his name was added to the growing Missing in Action list. Theresa vowed to keep those letters in her nightstand until Henry came home.

Seeing the envelopes reminds Theresa of Henry's last days home before the draft sent him to war. That cold, dreary December of 1968, they had spent every minute together. Theresa and Henry saw the new Monty Python movie, went to dinner at the local Howard Johnson's. Another night they stayed home, listening to records. Henry played the Rolling Stones "Honky Tonk Woman" and teased Theresa when she picked the Archie's hit record "Sugar, Sugar." They celebrated Richard Nixon's election and dreamed of their future.

Henry encouraged Theresa to continue with nursing school during his tour. "I'll be back in a year. When I get home my job at the mill will be waiting for me. We can buy a house, start our family." He kissed away his wife's tears. "Please watch over my parents, while I'm gone. I'll be home before you know it." Although it was a bittersweet Christmas, they tried to celebrate the holiday and exchanged gifts. A pearl necklace for Theresa, an engraved lighter for Henry.

The next September, chaplains knocked on Theresa's door. His fighter jet was shot down. A fiery crash, no recovery. Henry was declared Missing in Action. Theresa's life changed that day, she carried on the best she could. Finished nursing school, found a job in the local VA hospital, watched over Henry's parents, and leaned on her family for support. The years crawled by. Friends got married, had babies. She hid her broken heart behind smiles.

Judy Driscoll Winchenbaugh
Rockland, ME

Time passed, Nixon was re-elected in 1972. He pledged to bring the troops home. Anti-war protests were growing across the country, becoming increasingly violent. Theresa's patients at the VA were getting younger as the draft sent more young men into battle. Walker Cronkite shared news clips of battles on the nightly news. Henry's favorite team, the Miami Dolphins, won the Super Bowl in 1973. The letters from Henry were still in Theresa's nightstand, the elastic becoming brittle.

Then in January of that year, the Paris Peace Accord was signed, raising the hopes that the Vietnam War would soon be over. The next month, five hundred POWs were released and returned to the United States. Theresa scoured the list of names in the newspaper, but Henry's name wasn't there.

She watched John McCain being carried off the plane of returning POWs, shocked at his skeletal appearance. Happy for their families, a tiny corner of her heart was bitter that Henry wasn't on that plane.

The burglary of a Washington hotel in 1972 soon turned into the Watergate Scandal. Newspapers reported the burglars were hired to steal secrets of the Democratic Presidential Campaign. The scandal pushed aside the war in Vietnam, as more politicians including the US Attorney General were accused of taking part in the scandal. Theresa thought about Henry, how devastated he would be that Nixon was also being implicated in the scandal and accused of trying to stop the investigation.

Then on March 3, 1973, the POWs were back in the news. Hanoi released what they said were the last of their prisoners of war. The American Government flew them to the Philippines for medical attention on their way back home to Dover Air Force Base. Again, Henry's name was not on the list of returning POWs. The letters from Henry remained in the nightstand drawer.

Then Theresa received another visit from the Army chaplains.

Judy Driscoll Winchenbaugh
Rockland, ME

The chaplains explained to her there was a mix-up on some of the returning POW's names. A Wally Henley was listed as being on the plane. However, the Army had no record of that name ever serving. During interviews at Clark Air Force Base, it was discovered the captors had mistakenly transposed and changed the name of Henry Wallace to Wally Henley.

So after all these years, Theresa removes the elastic from the bundle of letters and reads them one last time. Tomorrow she is being flown to Dover Air Force Base. Theresa's Henry is going to walk off that plane.

***

The next year Theresa and Henry cuddle on the couch watching President Nixon's resignation speech while little Susie sleeps in her crib. The nightstand drawer in their bedroom is now empty. The letters Henry wrote to Theresa while in Vietnam are now packed in boxes in the attic, along with his uniform and military papers. Henry's Purple Heart is framed and proudly hung in the living room.

***

Sylvia Little-Sweat
Wingate, NC

Mates

Cardinals nesting
In the Nandina bushes—
Matador and Cape

Karen E. Wagner
Hudson, MA

When the Leaves Leave the Trees

It's easier in summer when
nature wears more clothes.
I slip between sheaves
of grain. Cornfields block
me from view.

Maybe I'll fade into the ranks
of uniformed school children.
No one sees me anymore.

I wait for autumn. I'll be
that bright crimson
orange amid the myriad
of gray-brown garb.
Anonymity is not my best
trait after all.

I excel as my original self.

As casually as leaves glide
from trees, poets sigh
when their words twirl,
caught in wind swirls
before settling. Wrought
through the juggernaut
of literary obstructions.

Karen E. Wagner
Hudson, MA

I'd gather those leaves
for a bonfire, drift
with curled smoke
bunches and puff into one.
From there I'd watch
the procession of leaves
from flared to debris.
And when they're dust
I'd turn back again
to those naked trees.

***

P. C. Moorehead
North Lake, WI

Madness

I can go out
and not come back.
I can go out and stay.

"She went for a walk,"
they'd say, "and never returned."

I can go out
and not come back,
but I won't.

I'm here.
I'll stay.

Bunny L. Richards
Trescott Twp., ME

February

Crows attack cracked corn
breath visible,
trees pop, branches creak.

Snow's cold white sheath
on black wires
overburdened again.

Thin-armored birches
with broken limbs
beckon plow drivers.

Watch out.

That mailbox is
in the way,
its red flag flaunts.

Quick work for a bright blade.

***

Before the Storm

Going down the street
Into the woods
Had enough of talking this week
Gonna put on an easy face
Catch some twigs between my teeth
And think about
No work in New York.

Graydon Dee Hubbard
St. George, UT

The Duchess Run

Here, give my weary spirits rest,
and raise my low-pitch'd thoughts
above Earth
or what poor mortals love.
—Izaak Walton

She probes heavier currents ahead of her with a stout, cherrywood wading staff. Satisfied, she edges deeper into a long glide and gingerly adjusts her footing. The bottom feels more secure now, and she listens intently.

She knows that smaller trout, when surface feeding, make greedy, slurping sounds—sounds that remind her of her father feasting on Yorkshire pudding. Paradoxically, the dainty sipping of larger trout is barely detectable, even to her sensitive ears. *Like my mother taking tea*, she thinks. Then she giggles. *How shocked they would be with such an undignified comparison. I'm surprised my brother didn't think of it. He was the shocking one.*

She rarely thinks of her childhood. So long ago in time. But not in mind, where memories preserve her youth as fresh as yesterday. As a schoolgirl in post-Edwardian England, she had even known the king and his family.

***

The chalk stream winding through her family's ancestral estate had always fascinated her. First with a small girl's natural fear of mysterious, dark and swirling waters. Then with a younger sister's indulged curiosity for the sport that preoccupied her brother, Richard. And finally with a vibrant young woman's passion for outdoor places, which perplexed her parents, delighted her brother, frustrated would-be suitors, and made her a recurring truant from confining classrooms,

Graydon Dee Hubbard
St. George, UT

endless Anglican Sunday litanies, and even the society of her class.

She fished for brown trout then. Richard showed her how to cast a dry fly and risked a sound thrashing by taking her to the stream when it was still forbidden territory for her. A most peculiar, awkward and inefficient way to catch a fish, she thought at first. Casting a long bamboo rod tired her, and she envied Richard's effortless style. For long hours, she practiced secretly on manicured estate lawns behind hedgerows that radiated from the manor house like protective fortress walls. But she couldn't make the line behave properly. It kinked in the reel. It fell in a tangled snarl just beyond her feet. Teasingly, it nipped at her long golden curls. It snared vagrant shrubs behind her. Scandalizing the gardeners, she shrieked at her rod and line, using the colorful epithets that occasionally slipped from Richard's lips. Her sunburned, freckled features contorted into a frown of intense determination. She persisted. Gradually her skills improved, and she transferred her practice to the stream. Wary trout responded, abandoning their instinctive caution. They seemed magically drawn, as if she cast a spell rather than one of Richard's discarded surface flies.

"Duchess, you're bewitching the fish," her brother teased. "It's not fair."

***

Hah, she thinks, *I could present a fly better than all of them—my father's estate warden, the bailiffs in County Dorset, even the poachers, eventually even Richard. It was concentration, which my brother taught me, and instinctive placement in anticipation of a rise, that canny prescience which cannot be taught. I've always had it. Even now. Age has stolen my sight, but not my foresight.*

Age cannot steal what I see here...in my mind. When I stand motionless and hear the trout begin to rise, I see a hun-

Graydon Dee Hubbard
St. George, UT

dred dimpling surface rings. When an eagle cries, I see him soaring high above me, a tireless sentinel of the sky who never rests. And when I hear a songbird sing, I see a feathery patchwork quilt of colors, stitched with all the rainbow's hues, flitting gaily from sunlight into shadow and back to sunlight again.

Age cannot change what I feel here...in my heart. Though my body is tired and worn, here my spirit soars fresh and strong, just as it did half-a-century ago. I'm welcomed here as an honored guest. I belong here, a restless young girl disguised as a sightless old woman and given an extra day of grace in this timeless place...to pose in a portrait of harmony that knows no age.

Richard, how I miss your presence! More than the husband I knew for a few short months. The other Richard, your namesake and only son of my daughter, is here with me. Every June he comes. He cheers me so...as you once did. He makes me laugh and feel like a young girl again...as you always did. He does not have your skills with a rod, nor mine. But still he comes...to be my eyes in springtime.

A voice breaks her reverie and returns her to the moment. "Duchess, you're slipping. It's some time into the rise now, and you haven't noticed. I've spotted a hungry trout for you."

"Thanks Richard," she sighs. "I'm afraid I've been daydreaming again. It always happens here. Now, where's that trout?"

"About 40 feet across and maybe ten feet upstream. Your backcast is clear."

"Good. A cast I can manage. There, I hear him. What's he rising to? Can you tell?"

"Pale morning dun, I think. Yes, he's after the infrequens, Duchess. You're casting the right pattern." Richard wades a few yards from his grandmother, staying to her left away from her casting arm, but close enough to support her if she needs it—which she seldom does. Amazed at her quickness

Graydon Dee Hubbard
St. George, UT

with the old bamboo rod, he watches as she expertly lengthens her casts and, without hesitation, gently deposits an artificial dun a precise 18 inches in front of the feeding fish. The fly drifts naturally down a narrow feeding lane until a shadowy bulge betrays a disdainful trout's approach and denial. Richard chuckles. "You enticed a refusal but no strike."

"Bloody snobbish fish," she scolds. "Must be Lord Nelson. He's a haughty one, but I pricked him good yesterday. I suspect he'll go down for a sulk. Anything else, Richard?"

"Across the creek. Next to the bank there's a fish. Very large, I think. He's feeding regularly, but I doubt you can reach him."

"Yes, I hear him. It's that mannerless glutton, Falstaff. I've caught him so many times he stays outside my casting limits. I'll wait until he moves into more productive feeding lanes. He will eventually. He's a fat and lazy lout. Can't resist an easy feed. Isn't that like a rainbow! Not like our brown trout in County Dorset. They were crafty fish. Never let hunger defeat their caution."

"You're uncanny, Duchess. You know the trout better than they know themselves."

She laughs. "Ah yes, patience exploits greed every time."

As predicted, the wait is short. The fish is deftly struck, played with a master's touch and guided into Richard's net. "My other Richard would never gillie for me," she muses. "He always made me net my catch, even when I was very small." Cradling her rod in her left arm, she runs her right hand down the leader and touches the subdued trout. "Is it Falstaff, Richard? A portly cockfish with sagging belly?"

"Must be Duchess. He's a paunchy brute."

Richard gently releases Falstaff to his grandmother's admonition, "Go on you bug-stuffed exaggeration of a foolish trout. Go back to your bankside lair out of casting range. May you stay forever free from less charitable anglers, sip size ten mayflies by the swarm every day, and as your namesake, live to an over-indulged and corpulent old age."

The morning hatch wanes, and they luncheon on a sun-drenched hillside where bees and butterflies prospect a few blossoms remaining from May's wildflower explosion. They rest, talk and wait. But there is no afternoon hatch. Placid waters appear deceptively lifeless, as aquatic insects stubbornly refuse to emerge, except for blue-bodied damsel flies who buzz the creek surface, daring lethargic trout to expand their customary food dimensions a hundred fold.

"Disappointed, Duchess?" Richard asks.

"Not really," she says. "I tire easily these days. Although I still enjoy the fishing, there is so much more. Please be my eyes and tell me what you see."

Richard is accustomed to being vision surrogate. It's part of their annual ritual. It pleases him to rekindle a sparkle in his grandmother's eyes, defying sightlessness. "There. Downhill. Two Orioles, I think, are darting about. They've found an insect hatch that..."

"Describe them to me," she interrupts impatiently.

"A mated pair. One has brilliant plumage; he must be the male. Golden-yellow body with black wings ribbed and edged in white. Bright carmine head with a yellow beak. Maybe seven inches long and indescribably beautiful in flight—like a dancing kaleidoscope. The female is camouflage green, a little darker on top."

"Yes! Yes!" She claps her hands in delight. "It's my Western Tanagers. They're back again—Lord Byron and Lady Annabella. He's such a beauty. I've always wondered why nature reversed for birds the appearance comparisons often made of human mates. Perhaps the male is the dandy of the sexes."

"Duchess, you're an incurable romantic," Richard chuckles. "Mother Nature protects her species by making the female less visible and therefore less vulnerable to natural predators, particularly when nesting."

"Something she forgot to do when she turned to

humans?" laughs the Duchess. "Now, what else do you see?"

"A Marsh Hawk who's protecting your favorite run from intruders. He's swooping on two fishermen wading downstream."

"It's Cromwell. That arrogant rascal. The aristocrat of the creek. Thinks he owns it all. He knows I won't put up with his tyrannous behavior." Rising, she removes a golden bandanna from her long white hair and snaps it above her head, stamping her feet impatiently. "Fly away Cromwell. They're only harmless fishermen."

Responding to her displeasure, Cromwell abandons his harassment of the beleaguered pair and glides off in search of smaller prey.

Other birds gather as if to welcome the Duchess: Evening Grosbeaks, Lazuli Buntings, even a Bullock's Oriole. A myriad of feathered creatures soon fill the hillside with their happy chatter. "Like my neighbors exchanging local gossip," she observes. Downstream where the creek widens into a marsh, a troop of Yellow-headed Blackbirds squawks in distant cacophony. "Clamoring for attention, like a gathering of all your rejected hostesses and discarded suitors," teases Richard.

The Duchess dozes with her memories.

***

Richard was right. She was always popular in the valley. Despite her infrequent acceptance, valley parties begged her attendance, as hostesses competed for social standing, particularly in winter when skiing brought many visitors from far off, important places. They sought status and satisfaction of vanity in securing a guest who could be introduced by a name with royal implications. Her title was part of her English birthright, and it annoyed her to have what she considered an affectionate nickname exploited for social gain.

And the suitors! Yes, there had been many—an endless

procession. All eager to comfort a beautiful English war widow who embodied the eternal youth and freshness of an untrammeled soul. A famous novelist with a home in the valley pursued an intermittent but ardent courtship into middle age. Together they fished the creek in spring, when she embarrassed him with her superior skill and angered him with her scorn at killing trout. Reluctantly, she returned with him on fall hunts. Although she was a better shot, she generally refused to hold a gun. Killing so many wildfowl seemed brutal and wanton to her.

"How can an admired author deal with human life with such sensitivity and perception, but be so callous and unfeeling toward God's lesser creatures?" she criticized.

Sometimes he refused to be angered by her criticism. "I contrive the nature of my characters," he responded with a roguish grin, "not because human species are so worthy of greater respect, but because I must earn a living. Killing fish and birds is necessary so that I may eat, when my hard-earned royalties have all been squandered on profligate living, particularly in the company of a long-legged, golden-tressed, sharp-tongued, unkempt English wench who pretends to royal descent and fancies she can outdo a man in his favorite sporting pursuits."

She matched him in wit as well as in sport and continued with mock hostility. "It's only a simple-minded English wench who could suffer the company of an ill-mannered, self-admiring, bandy-legged, bristle-faced, whiskey-sodden, gut-swollen, brutish prig of peasant heritage, whose public would desert him if they knew of his deceit, and who must kill lesser creatures to establish his superiority. And the problem with eating is one of too much eating, and also of dubious talent and diminished capacity, which naturally results in a decreasing royalty—certainly not of squandering, for, unless there is another deluded English wench involved, your indulgence of me is barely more than miserly."

Their quarrel disintegrated into laughter.

Graydon Dee Hubbard
St. George, UT

They shared a mutual distaste for social posturing and affectation. On a warm spring evening when they abdicated their party celebrity status, they drove to where an old dirt road crossed the creek. While other valley residents clustered for cocktails, mindless conversation, and elegant dining, they picnicked a light supper of wine, salami, and cheese. Through twilight lingering after an evening storm, they shared a splendid English brandy from her wine cellar and maintained a steady badinage until a majestic valley sunset halted conversation. As last rays from a dying sun broke free from low-lying clouds, they watched a vast panorama no painter could capture in a single canvas. For a fleeting moment, before far western plains fully embraced the sun, nearby fields of young barley dazzled their eyes with a wet emerald glow, as fresh green growth glistened against luminous amber backlighting. Treeless foothills undulated north into Idaho's Pioneer Mountains and metamorphosed from drab brown into an artist's color study of soft lavenders and bright purples, with shadowy intervening shades. Then the stream burst into life as hundreds of rising trout cleansed the creek of thousands of dying insects. When the feeding frenzy ended, the creek surface shone in twilight like fresh-polished silver. It was a scene he'd never written, a scene she'd never view again, but one she could still imagine more than sight could ever comprehend.

***

Richard breaks the long silence. "You're unusually quiet, Duchess. You seem to be more contemplative this spring."

"Just remembering," she sighs. "Or perhaps only mind-wandering into my past. I've been doing a lot of that lately, as if I'm permitted one last visit to each year of my life. I dream of my family's estate in England, of the ever-smiling face of my brother, of another chalk stream...so much like this one, and its bright-spotted trout; of the terrible war that

Graydon Dee Hubbard
St. George, UT

took both husband and brother." She pauses, and, with a deliberate toss of her head, arrests a darker mood before it can advance. Her features brighten, as she turns to feel sunlight full upon her face.

"But mostly I dream of here...of this place I've learned to love with a depth of feeling I can neither fully understand nor fairly explain...an emptiness of words which so often accompanies a fullness of heart. I dream of stillness in a crisp morning sunrise, of solitude, of impatient anticipation...such a deliciously painful fret, an almost physical need...waiting for the day's first strike; of my creature friends who've suffered the silly English names I've given them. Here my restless spirit finally rests at sunset, when my favorite landscape speaks to me with muted sounds more peaceful than the music of Handel or any of the masters.

"And I dream of springtime attention from a grandson who still cannot fish very well despite all I've tried to teach him, and who brings me here to reassure a sightless, white-haired English lass that she can still be young and see again!"

Now laughing again, she seeks her grandson's arm. "Come, Richard. Take me home. I'm being far too serious, and I don't want to spoil your holiday."

"Duchess, please return with me. To the city. It's time you left the valley."

"No, Richard." She's adamant. "I'll never leave the valley, although I think this may be my last summer here. And I can't abandon my valley guides. After you've gone, they come. Each week one brings me here. Like you, they spoil me so. I don't know why!"

"It's your wine cellar," Richard laughs. "They conspire to drink it dry."

"I know it's not the meager fare I provide for lunch. But they do love my wine."

"And they're all in love with you, Duchess." Richard grips her hands. "You've always enchanted the valley guides. They see in you what they can't find in younger women. You have more genuine passion for life than most of the valley belles. The guides all marvel at your courage and how you still bewitch the trout. They hope someday to learn your secrets."

***

It is, as she foresaw, the Duchess's last summer.

***

In the new spring of a new year, Richard and the valley guides gather where an old dirt road still wanders through rolling hills and crosses the creek. The air is frosty cool, and trout are spawning. Crimson-sided males flaunt their seasonal colors. A Marsh Hawk hovers forlornly overhead. The fishermen bring no rods, only a hand-lettered wooden memorial which they imbed firmly in a streamside knoll.

STAND QUIETLY A MOMENT
FOR THIS IS THE DUCHESS RUN
THE PLACE SHE LOVED BEST
HERE HER SPIRIT ROAMS—FOREVER FREE
CLOSE YOUR EYES AND SENSE HER PRESENCE
IMAGINE THE THINGS SHE SAW THAT WE CANNOT
FEEL HER TOUCH IN THE CARESS OF THE MIDDAY BREEZE
HEAR HER LAUGHTER IN THE WARBLER'S SONG

That spring the entire valley mourns.

First published in *Cutthroat, A Journal of the Arts.*

Robert B. Moreland
Pleasant Prairie, WI

Hardwoods

Can you know someone
unless you see them naked,
and vulnerable?

Stalwart oaks limbs bare,
maples blush red, disrobing,
shy weeping willows.

Slender, lithe elms reach;
buxom ash trees full bodied,
white birch stark, nimble.

Shagbark hickory
unclothed glory, slowly sways,
bounty squirreled away.

Death promising life
cold winter portraying harsh
resurrected truths.

***

P. C. Moorehead
North Lake, WI

Wanting

Street peace,
that's what I want—
a street of peace,
an avenue of joy.

Abby Staberg
Brunswick, ME

A Walk Before Winter

It is late in the day
we are late in our years
the windshield lets in light
from a scant November sun

Let's walk I say
so you park the car on the side of the road
just shy of a ditch
we are at the edge
of a woodsy path we've never walked before
with all its implications

First past the trailhead
you scan the barks of trees for splashes of yellow
the painted promise
of a destination worth pursuing

One behind the other
we walk without words
confident on paths heaped with pine needles
careful around menacing roots
that are gnarly as arthritic hands

Just off the path we spy a pond
and yield to the impulse to skip some stones

Under a sky of storm clouds conspiring
our reflections wobble on the wind-stroked surface
undaunted we inhale all that was blue
now turning bleak

Abby Staberg
Brunswick, ME

There are tree limbs protruding at water's edge
we dance a jaunty two-step around them
with spirits like passion fruit fresh off the vine
we are buoyant as light

***

Prayer at Still Waters

Earth's oceans and rivers and streams form the lifeblood
that flows through our bodies
like truth through a lie.

Each breath that we breathe is a swallow of promise;
its pungent aroma
the flavor of sky.

A taste of tomorrow seeps up through the soil
to season the leaves
as they dance in the breeze.

The act of forgetting awakens remembrance.
While we whisper *thank you*
the earth pulsates *please.*

Thomas Fallon
Rumford, ME

Two Friends

John and Lisa sat at Dee's for
their usual morning coffee.

"With the snow Christmas
was better this year," John said.

Lisa didn't reply. She sipped
her coffee.

"More snow than we had last
year," John said. "And with
two new grandkids, whew!"

"I guess," Lisa said quietly.

"Everyone show up at your
house," John asked.

Lisa didn't reply.

John sipped his coffee.

Then he said slowly, "Quiet
at yours, hunh...?"

Lisa didn't reply.

Then she said quietly.
"Mother wasn't there."

John was quiet.

Thomas Fallon
Rumford, ME

Then he slowly reached
for her hand.

They held hands.

***

Cordula Mathias
Trevett, ME

Counting Sixteenths in ¾ Time

Find your rhythm
ta fa te fe
ta fa te fe

Keep on counting
On the down beat
ta fa te fe

ta fa te fe
Make your life count
Tempus fugit

ta fa te fe
ta fa te fe
Play the next bar

Play it solo
ta fa te fe
ta fa te fe

ta fa te fe
ta fa te fe
Keep on going

Roselyn Stewart
Brookfield, WI

Morning

In the stillness of the morning
I watch as shafts of sunlight
stream through green leafy trees.
They play upon the grass below.
A cloudless powder blue sky
provides a backdrop for the
canopy of green trees.
I sit sipping my coffee and drink
in my surroundings. I crave this
timeout at the start of the day as
nature sooths my pensive mood.
Reluctantly I leave my peaceful
oasis and retire to my kitchen
where I sit writing a poem.
I observe my upstairs neighbor
walk past my patio door on his way
to retrieve his mail and I realize
it's time for me to do the same.
As I open my mail and leave behind
the serenity of my morning I hope
my interlude with nature will give me
the strength to face the remainder of
my day.

Judy O'Dell
Rockport, ME

Being Brave

In a *New York Times* story, I read that our new Supreme Court judge, Ketanji Brown Jackson, was a star on her high school debate team. Her specialty was oratory, and she "learned how to reason and how to write." I was impressed by her bravery in allowing her name to be placed in nomination, knowing what obstacles she would face. I tuned in to some of the confirmation hearings, paying attention to her demeanor and presentation skills. Watching her triggered my memories of being on the forensics team in ninth grade at Towson Catholic High School.

Sister Theodore, the moderator of the forensics team and my Latin teacher, recruited me. I wish I knew what she'd seen in me so early in my first semester of high school. I had hoped to make the basketball team, but that was not likely for a ninth-grader. So, when I learned that she had also recruited Teddy, a boy I had a crush on, I agreed to join the team, knowing we would spend time together at meetings. The team competed with the other Baltimore Catholic high schools on the first Saturday of the month throughout the school year.

At our first team meeting, the seniors told us about the various categories in the competition: extemporaneous, impromptu, declamation, original oratory, and debate. Sister asked me to try extemporaneous, where you are given a short news article to read, have fifteen minutes to prepare, and then deliver a five-minute speech. It was October 1962, and the Cuban Missile Crisis, the opening of the Second Vatican Council, Russian spy satellites, and James Meredith's enrollment as the only African American at the University of Mississippi were the headline news stories. These were confusing topics for a fourteen-year-old. Both the *Baltimore Morning Sun* and the *Evening Sun* were delivered to our house. I always read the comics before the headlines. Now I would need to read and understand the news stories, since I would not know what would be assigned in the competition.

For practice, Sister gave me a story about a bill pending in Congress that would add the phrase "so help me God" to the US armed forces enlistment and promotion oaths. As a lifelong Catholic school student, I didn't know anyone who did not believe in God, and I couldn't understand why this was controversial. My five-minute presentation lasted 30 seconds and was something like: I don't know why this is an issue; we already pledge allegiance to one nation under God and swear on a Bible in court. Sister suggested that I try original oratory instead. Students prepare an eight-minute speech, memorize and present it at the competitions. But what should I write?

I was one of the few older children in our suburban Baltimore neighborhood full of baby-boom kids and was an in-demand babysitter. Their parents like to stay out late, and I absorbed the black and white movies that were televised at 11 PM when the regular programming ended. I was fascinated by World War II movies, especially those about the military nurses captured during the war in the Philippines. I watched *So Proudly We Hail* with Claudette Colbert, Paulette Goddard, and Veronica Lake, *Corregidor* with Elissa Landi and Otto Kruger, and *Cry Havoc* with Margaret Sullavan, Ann Southern, and 11 other actresses. At the end of *They Were Expendable*, I cried when the John Wayne character's good-bye phone call to his nurse love interest, Donna Reed's character, was cut off. He boarded the last flight out of the Philippines, leaving nurse Donna Reed to face internment. When the TV went off the air for the night, I sat staring at the blank screen, wondering if I could ever be as brave as those nurses.

Women were the heroes in these movies.

I had found an idea for my speech. Sister Theodore told me it was an odd topic but encouraged me to write it. My mother and my father had served in the Navy during World War II. My mother was not a nurse but a court reporter in the 4th Naval District General Court Martial. I listened when they and my uncles, who had served in the army, told stories. Writing about war did not seem unusual to me.

I wish I had saved a copy of the speech. I recall spending time in the Towson Library researching the war in the Philippines from microfilmed newspapers. There was not much written about the nurses after their capture, but I learned that when the Japanese occupied the hospitals on Corregidor and Bataan, they were surprised to see women in uniform. The news of the capture of those nurses spurred other nurses to volunteer to serve. My speech opened with some dramatic sentences about the Japanese invasion of the Philippines in 1942 and General MacArthur and his family fleeing Corregidor in a PT boat, vowing to return. It included what I imagined the captured army and navy nurses faced as prisoners of war, caring for the other prisoners despite shortages of food and medicine, and how their senior officers maintained military order and discipline to keep up morale until they were liberated in 1945. It was probably full of words like bravery, courage, resilience, and patriotism. Most likely, it was an amalgam of the scripts for the movies I watched. Sister Alma, my English teacher, helped with edits, and I practiced in front of a mirror in my bedroom until I memorized it.

On the Friday before the first competition, Sister Theodore suspended Latin and had the team make their presentations before the class. Teddy had selected impromptu, where he was given a sentence, had five minutes to prepare and then gave a two-minute speech using the sentence. He was brilliant. I was not. My hands shook, my voice was atonal, and I looked at the ceiling as I recited what I had memorized, worried that I would forget. Sister asked me to stay after school so she could coach me. She underlined the passages that called for more expression in my voice, and I prac-

Judy O'Dell
Rockport, ME

ticed over and over. I had memorized and recited many poems in grade school but had never faced a competition. She told me to think of it as a tied score basketball game where I was on the free-throw line with 15 seconds left, and I made the shot.

Our team gathered with students from the other schools in the auditorium at Calvert Hall College High School on Saturday morning. We received our classroom assignments based on our categories, and I found myself in a room with twelve other students, all older than me. The three judges, whom we understood to be teachers, sat in the back of the room with scoring sheets in front of them. We drew numbered slips of paper, and I was number 7. My hands started to sweat. I was so jittery I could not pay attention to the others' speeches. Finally, it was my turn. I stated my name, high school, and the speech's title and began. I forced myself to look at the audience, forgot where I was supposed to change the expression in my voice, but survived the eight minutes without stumbling. I gratefully slunk back into my chair.

I came in 12 out of 12. My score sheet said although my speech was interesting, I looked scared, and my delivery was poor. I didn't care. I was just happy it was over. Teddy was 7th in his round, and we consoled each other. Despite my poor performance, our team came in third. As the season went on, I watched how the older students presented and learned how to vary the tone of my voice. I edited the speech to make it more dramatic. Thanks to Sister Theodore's continued coaching, my scores improved, but I never won my category. At the end of the school year, Sister told me that I had done well for a freshman in a competitive category and would do better next year.

My father's company transferred us to Philadelphia, and we moved that summer. Leaving my friends behind and entering a new high school in tenth grade was traumatic, but my forensics team experience boosted my self-confidence. I was sorry that my new high school did not have a forensics

Judy O'Dell
Rockport, ME

team, but I did play basketball for three years and earned a varsity letter.

I have made many presentations in my career as a CPA. At large conferences where there were 500 people in the audience, my face was projected on TV screens around the room. Before beginning every presentation, I would think of Sister Theodore, pretend I was on the free-throw line, and remind myself to smile so I would not look scared.

***

Steve Troyanovich
Florence, NJ

when the sky weeps...

sometimes the night's sky weeps
with the stars as its tears
—John Trudell

weary stars shiver
in a cold sadness
nearing tomorrow's embers
of widowing dawn...

plunging into the embrace
of your fleeting being
eternity is only yesterday's moment
igniting the undressed chill
of still another day...

Brandon Ying Kit Boey
Falmouth, ME

Pond Ice

In Memoriam

We stretched the tarp before the days and nights grew cold,
so you could skate
When the water turned to ice.
It was hard and grey, and smoky white when it finally froze,
How you children filled the yard then.
But the ice was not yet solid,
And when it cracked, the blades of the boots sank deep,
Piercing the plastic through.
Had it stayed as cold the pond would have mended,
Its shards may have hardened and closed its cracks.

From the swinging-rope tree, you fell—
The sun at the last zenith in the summer.
They said you did not feel a thing when you landed
Before sinking beneath the river's current.
Those children waited for you for many hours,
Still you did not emerge.

I think about how all the water ran out from the ice pond
when the cold receded,
Away into the ground.
Everyone feels loss some time, they told us,
Just not how deep it really goes.
Each day we waited for a freezing again,
Filling the pond with the water,
Hoping it would hold.

Now at night we wait for ice,
So thick a layer this time
That steel will not pierce it,
On a tarp that is stretched
too thin.

Rebecca Brooks
Topsham, ME

August Won't Remember Your Favorite Color

A daffodil nudges through
the blackberry-winter ground
and leans into the fickle rays of light.
Clouds have conquered the sky real estate.
This struggle creates a rumination
of August and you.

Of a lakeside day warmed by the sun
with loved ones celebrating each other.
How courageous of you
to stand beside us once again,
poised with a quiet grace.
In your hands, a small indigo-pottery plate
cradled two treasured gold bands.
Your hair had started growing back.
while mine took on your cherished
halcyon hue.
You claimed I wore it well, so I kept it.

Outside my window, under the emerging dawn
crocuses skirt the forest edge.
I admire the goldfinch
perched on the feeder
seemingly carefree and blithe.
Suddenly it occurs to me.
I never cared for saffron shades
until August disappeared.

E. M. Barsalou
East Kingston, NH

North Star and Horizon

Blanketing in the timberline
A cold mist of the so sublime
Eerily entranced over the lake
Blackness consumes all life that's awake.
The moon lapses through the clouds,
Moving in shapes of faces with fright;
Evil alluring, dismal traces of night.
For this reason of being and embracing—
A shudder effect, a shivering of the skin;
These faces of haste, out in the darkness—
A shrill consuming my soul left in thrills—
Of how I mistake the loneliness I enstate
Out here in the old winters of cold moonlit
Theories conspire; turning everything into
Direness out of conscience and reprisal;
You made your way through like a compass
Infused, unholy compassion in its entrance:
Of the North Star Horizon...leading you back!!

***

Sylvia Little-Sweat
Wingate, NC

Forsythia

Along dormant stems
March lights the voltage of Spring—
In Sunshine yellow

Richard Manichello
Baltimore, MD

A Single Shell

He took the sleek mahogany boat from the steel rack, easing it gently down onto his shoulders. Down the ramp, and onto the weathered planks at the river's edge, the pure solace of the ritual gave him an awareness of place and history. The river at daybreak filled him with a sense of wonder. From the launch dock he could see the iron arches of Strawberry Mansion Bridge, the filigree of intricate spokes and crossbeams catching the first rosy hues of dawn light. A pair of Canada geese, skimming low across the surface of the water, searched for a landing spot along the green banks of West River Drive. The stone Parthenon of the Art Museum, several leagues downriver, was at this hour but a dense geometry of silhouetted shapes against the pale sky.

Eakins must have seen this, these sights, this peace and beauty, must have felt these same impressions here when he painted. He envied Eakins, Max Schmitt, the Biglins—envied their inertia. Things stood still for them. The pictures in his mind couldn't be kept or stored, or stopped. Dreamers are powerless painters. Tomorrow would be different. This special hour, on this morning, connected him too fervently with one fleeting spirit. The river's enduring movement mirrored his wish for steadfast love and constancy. And tomorrow, she'd be gone.

A strong breeze churned the grey waters. It looked like a Parisian boulevard of smooth, rounded cobblestone. Small whitecaps spilled into pewter troughs the waves made, and the broad surface rippled and sallied easterly across the flow. He set the boat into the dockside chop and tipped oars. Today the row would be strenuous, the strain redoubled with the prospect of her departure.

Twelve-stroke for the first quarter-mile, enough for starters. Warming, getting loose. Upriver to the bridge.

Richard Manichello
Baltimore, MD

Stroke. Rest. Muscle and pain into Stroke, thoughts of her into Rest.

***

"Why, Ali, why must it be this way? You can't go."

"I must go, darling." She pressed and pleaded. "This is a duty I have, a duty I feel. Surely, you can understand."

"No, I can't. For the life of me, I cannot understand this impulsiveness."

"Impulse? You don't understand, do you?"

She turned away from him.

"It's not your fight, we can't help everybody with their problems," he said, rationally. "Really, what is there to understand?"

"Oh, please, David. Don't be pedestrian. You're so pragmatic sometimes."

"You know what I mean, Ali. You were born here in the States. You're a full-blooded American. You don't owe anyone. You know what I mean."

"That's funny. Aren't we all just worldly transplants? I thought only Native Americans were full-blooded Americans, and look at what we did to them."

"They won't let you fight. You think you're going to be on the front lines, but you could be killed just the same... for doling-out chicken soup, or giving someone a blood transfusion. Wouldn't that be heroic?"

"Don't David." She leveled a stern look through her thick black eyebrows. "Don't be insensitive. I'm a nurse. I have skills and training. Helping is fighting. Doing something is heroic."

Set the rhythm. *Sixteen-stroke.* The perspiration began to run beneath his scalp, streaming down across his forehead and face. From beneath his arms, soaking his flanks, the wetness flowed freely. His back burst with pain as rhythm and beat increased. *Take it up to twenty, against the current.*

Richard Manichello
Baltimore, MD

He could not grasp. He could not fathom Ali's selflessness in the face of possible death. The conflict in a land so remote seemed endless and dangerously unpredictable. A young, urban-American, upwardly mobile professional, Ali shared nothing other than sympathy with the fighting factions, even less with the issues and philosophies of the current revolution. Living together for almost four years, he wondered how he could have been so oblivious to her deepest loyalties. How could he have missed this, the importance of her work, her order of priorities, and his place in it?

A mile marker. The wind rolled over his back, tousled his hair around the temples and forehead; his vision fluttered at the periphery. *Stroke. Push. Pull into the wind.* The riggers screamed and rattled. His thighs burned, twisting and striating, they engorged with adrenalin and blood, pulsating with a syncopation to match his strokes. *Raise the rate. Twenty-two.* The sweat dripped from his nose steadily, down onto knees and shins and thighs, onto the throbbing meat of his exertion. The smooth lacquered prow sliced through the chop, parting the waters like a hunter's blade separating fresh kill.

He and Ali plied a mixed-double at Henley a year before. A Second, they managed, winning ribbons, cups, and citations. He licked the salt sweat from her shoulder and kissed her deeply at the finish that day in a shower of streamers and confetti.

Twenty-six. Rest. Glide. Turn downriver. The top of the bandshell in the park was barely visible. The river banks were green and mossy, unseen cars made that hollow speeding-whooshing sound on Kelly Drive. Downriver will be easier. It will be faster. The shell turns like a straw needle on a still black lake. *South. Set the rhythm. Set it.*

He remembered the Stotesbury Cup Regatta and looking at the moon from the roof of Vespers.

"Let's live together, Ali," he said, grabbing her about the waist.

Richard Manichello
Baltimore, MD

"Let's just look at the moon, David. Let's not muck-it-up. Please?"

"I love you, Ali. I want this. I want us to live together."

"David! Can we not complicate things?"

"No complications." He threw up his arms, dramatically. "Love is not complicated, darling."

"Love is impossible, David."

"Yes. And it happens all the time." She sauntered away from him, to the wooden railing.

"Have you tried the oysters? They're good," she said, brightly.

"Change the subject. That's it! That's your way."

"No really, on the half-shell. They're delicious. You're a single, David. I'm the other half. Between us, a pearl."

Their eyes met. He smiled at her, and the worth of their union hung there in the night air like the unmoving damp leaves of the oak trees overhead. Swaying in each other's arms that clear evening on the roof, she was lithe and fragile, mysterious, sensuous, and so lovely in the moonlight. She was brown, golden brown, from the sun. He wanted her forever. They'd each won a race that festive day on the river. Their embrace, coddled in several glasses of champagne, was slow and deliberate, and warm. Their caress was gentle and bubbly, bending to the fatigue of their accomplishments.

"Why did we fall in love, David?" she said, feigning reprimand, giggling. "Damn you, you silly goose! Why do two people fall in love, anyway?"

"Because assassins like to work in pairs," he said, mugging morbidly.

***

Twenty-eight to the new mark. Two-mile marker sailed past the hull. At racing speed, with the wind, he was flushed with the power and stress of each beat, spent by thoughts of Ali's abandonment. The slender shell tore through the water full-boar, spray topped the knife-like bow showering him in a steady drizzle. The Beats, like a metronome. The big stone piers of Railroad Bridge arched above him now, turning a great shadow on the wide waters, a timeless mortuary to the past. Columbia Bridge. Faster he rowed. Girard Avenue Bridge. He pulled and the boat leapt forward.

Shallow and silent his crimson-and-white oars coaxed the dark river back upstream. He was approaching the sleepy boathouses lining the east bank, the closed eyelids of their doors pulled down tight to the decks. The emblazoned shields and insignia of the clubs jutted from second-floor balconies. Names, carvings, waving burgees quivered and flashed their reflections on the water—Sedgeley, Penn, LaSalle, Drexel, Vespers. Black garage door windows watched him pass like cat's eyes.

Three-mile marker. Deeper. The catch was perfect. The spillway, just a half-mile beyond. Fairmount Water Works. The strong undercurrents near the spillway were dangerous and often inescapable, a torrent of rushing waters, whirlpools, narrow channels, and subsurface canals, and then, the dam.

"I'll write. I promise, I'll write, David. I'll tell you all about it. I'll keep a diary."

"Call when you arrive, will you? Please Ali."

"Yes, at the airport. I'm on a bus for the camp, directly. They don't give us much time... "

"You're my brave Ali, my courageous warrior. You'll take care of yourself, darling, be on-guard."

"What'll you do, David... tomorrow?"

"I'll miss you."

"No, you mustn't, you silly goose. Don't give me that thought to go away with. You'll go to the river and row, won't you? Of course you will, I know you will."

"Yes, yes, I'll go to the river. I promise. I'll row so hard, darling, I'll break all speed records. Twenty-eights past Vespers, like a rocket. Remember? Thirty past that big old

Richard Manichello
Baltimore, MD

frumpy museum."

Ali laughed. Her smile crushed a dream in him that was just beginning to bloom. They walked a few more steps to the jetway door, walking and embracing, and the distant voice of a flight attendant called for final boarding.

"I'll take the river right to the sea, Ali, all the way to the sea." He said, caressing her cheek lightly.

"You silly goose," she whispered. "Yes, and you'll fly over the dam, I suppose?"

He squeezed her hand in his.

"Now give us a kiss, Ali, one last kiss, darling. And off you go."

***

Steve Troyanovich
Florence, NJ

winter star

like the first star's footprint
memory returns
finding a winter rose
drenched in fading earth

Adele & Anthony D'Alessandro
Celebration, FL

A Living Nightmare

A cloudless and inviting Long Island sunrise massaged my face. I glanced at the grandfather clock, and vaulted out of bed. My wife Adele planned to start her new consulting business that morning and I decided to accompany her. She scheduled a 10 A.M. appointment in Brooklyn, New York.

Strolling toward my car, I took a deep breath. Despite a slight nip in the air, I scented the aroma of a summer beach day. Minutes later, I stopped at a local bakery to pick up breakfast. After my purchase, I nearly stumbled into our car while hugging freshly baked bagels. I yanked my nose out of that aromatic and crinkled paper bag and savored our wake-up coffee.

Pleasantly surprised by scattered, small clusters of traffic on the way to the city, I pressed my finger to the cassette recorder and listened to the rock band Bread's songs. Wearing a silly ear-to-ear grin, I raved to Adele about the wonderful day we'd begun to experience. Further on into our ride, we heard distant, scattered sirens, and noticed peculiar clouds. We didn't think anything of it. Despite these distractions, I expressed concern about our late arrival for her business meeting.

My cell phone blared. Our son Pete, a usually calm lawyer, called from his Washington, DC office with a slightly raised voice.

He asked, "Where are you?"

"In Brooklyn," I answered.

"Do you see anything unusual on the highway or sky?"

"Not really, perhaps a weird cloud, rumpled like an unmade bed," I said.

Adele looked over and noticed police cars flying by and also spotted smoke in the distant sky.

Pete raised his voice even more, "Get off at the closest

exit! Forget your business. Head back to Long Island. No questions, and turn your radio on!"

Listening to the radio, we heard many chilling and conflicting stories. Adele gently tapped my arm and I said, "You're so upset about what's happening."

She answered, "Of course I am; however, I wonder if you've become Mario Andretti?"

Nodding and apologizing, I eased off my gas pedal.

When we finally arrived home, the enormity of the tragedy faced us. I hung my keys behind the door as my telephone resounded. I answered the call with baited breath.

One of my closest friends Jay called to ask if I'd heard news of the Pentagon attack. "Pentagon attack?" I said with cracking voice. "Never heard about that." I mentioned that we'd just returned home. When he informed me that his son—an officer in the armed forces—was stationed at the Pentagon, I trembled and noticed goose pimples occupying my arms. I told him we'd pray for his boy.

While waiting to hear more about Jay's son, I plopped in my lounge chair, slowly wiped my moisture laden face, and then my fingernails began their tap dance. The rest of the afternoon images of smoldering buildings, fleeing people, screams and casualties commandeered the television. I shuddered.

Then, my friend Larry called from his college office and disclosed that his daughter, recognizing her lateness for work at the World Trade Center, decided to grab a cup of coffee on the street. That happened minutes before the attack. Ironically, that last-minute coffee stop saved her life. Her pop said, "I will never ever complain about her overuse of coffee. In fact, I will buy her the finest coffee maker ever made."

Hours later, my beleaguered friend Jay called to inform me his son had the day off from his Pentagon assignment. Two home runs in terms of lives saved. Watching the television, however, I realized that positive news would end soon.

The next day a sad, seemingly endless procession began.

Adele & Anthony D'Alessandro
Celebration, FL

We learned that two of my former high school students were trapped in the Towers. A popular local young man and sparkplug in our community and New York City police officer ran into the inferno to save lives. He never came out. Tragically, countless others were swallowed up in an evil jungle of fire, smoke, in a never-ending hellhole. Their lives, hopes, and dreams trampled in a flash. The list of casualties, about three thousand, included several of our friends and neighbors.

And so it began, within a week our tiny street choked with hearses and fire trucks transporting the victims and heroes to the local church, following a trail of sorrows. Several firefighters and police from our area were recipients of funeral mass blessings at parade's end. There were enough tears to flood the street. That scene was repeated for days, and hair raising shrieks were heard from some mourners. Drenched in the face of terrorizing history and listening to a swell of dirges, I became trapped in a cone of melancholy for over a month.

The murderous attack continued after the initial horror. Police, firefighters, and volunteers entered the conflagration during and after the sneak attack. Speaking to my good friend Lieutenant Gerry whom I privately referred to as Mr. Brave, grimaced when describing his leaps into the smoldering and sizzling pile of devastation and his discovery of wedding bands, charm bracelets, and human remains. Despite masks, both he and his courageous colleagues inhaled venomous fumes. These heroes worked countless hours in the hope of finding survivors.

Nine-eleven remained a part of them nearly a score of years later when they dealt with disease caused by terrorists. Unfortunately, our Mr. Brave finally succumbed to the toxic air delivered that fatal day. Our family lost him, one true blue, talented, courageous, and upstanding American cursed by the Nine-eleven terrorist attack.

In life, some scars and sores still hurt even though healed

Adele & Anthony D'Alessandro
Celebration, FL

or appearing healed. Baseball, yes baseball, helped resurrect my spirit at that time. For me, the World Series a month or so after the attack of terrorism captured a curative stage. Fans swelled in the Yankee Stadium seats. President Bush faced with numerous threats, jogged out to the baseball mound to throw out the first baseball. Before he hurled the ball, future Yankee Hall of Famer Derek Jeter said, "Mr. President, you'd better throw a strike or they'll boo you."

He pitched a perfect strike and Americans in attendance in person or on television that day swelled with patriotism and pride while casting politics aside. They chanted, "USA, USA, USA," triggering chills to run up and down my spine.

***

Patrick T. Randolph
Lincoln, NE

Mutual Respect

Fishing with my dad—
We pick a quiet trout stream,
Lose ourselves in thought;

Only the fish can hear our
Ideas surface for air.

GOOSE RIVER ANTHOLOGY, 2023

We seek selections of fine poetry, essays, and short stories (3,000 words or less) for the **21st annual** *Goose River Anthology, 2023.* The book will be beautifully produced with full color cover in both paperback and hardcover.

You may submit even if you have been published before in a previous edition of the *Goose River Anthology.* We retain one-time publishing rights. All rights revert back to the author after publication. You may submit as many pieces as you like.

EARN CASH ROYALTIES. Author will receive a 10% royalty on all sales that he or she generates.

There is no purchase required and nothing is required of the author for publication. Deadline for submissions is April 30, 2023. Publication will be in the fall of 2023 (they make great Christmas gifts). Guidelines are as follows:

- Submit clean, typed copy by snail mail—**Mandatory**
- Email a Word (prefered), rtf, or PDF file (if possible)
- Reading fee: $1.00 per page
- Do not put two poems on the same page
- Essays and short stories **must be** double-spaced
- **SASE (#10 or larger) for notification—Mandatory** (one forever stamp) plus additional postage for possible return of submission if desired.
- Author's name & address at top of each page of paper copy and **first page of emailed copies**.

Submit to:
Goose River Anthology, 2023
3400 Friendship Road
Waldoboro, ME 04572-6337
Email: gooseriverpress@gmail.com
www.gooseriverpress.com

www.ingramcontent.com/pod-product-compliance
Lightning Source LLC
Chambersburg PA
CBHW020630110726
47899CB00002B/723